Once again the enemy has been de
and the word of Betty's testimony! I
as a prayer partner on a mission t
how God was moving in Betty's life. I have watched over the years that have passed as God has redeemed what the enemy had stolen from Betty. This book brings glory to God's name as the reader sees a picture of God's faithfulness to her!

—Tilly Welborn
Pastor, Ebenezer United Methodist Church
Jefferson, Georgia

What a significant spiritual love story! Betty has shared her life story, which I think embodies the principle found in Romans 8:28: "And we know that all things work together for good to them that love God, to them who are the called according to his purpose." In Nothing Wasted Betty recalls many events... that God ultimately uses for good in her life and for those she has served.

Having known Betty since April 1981 in the lay witness ministry and having been teammates on numerous short-term mission trips, I am aware of her story and have heard many facets of it in the form of personal testimony. She is one of the most powerful witnesses for Jesus that I know. She has a sweet witness and a love for people. She also has ministry gifts and the availability to be highly effective for the Lord. As a lay witness mission coordinator since 1979 I realize the power of a personal testimony by laity in the life of individuals both in the church and in everyday situations.

Betty's book will witness and help every reader at many points as they identify with her and understand how God loves us and wants us to draw close to Him.

—Walter L. Boyd
Lay Witness Coordinator, United Methodist Church

I have never read a more beautiful love story, not only the love of a wife for her husband but a powerful love of a faithful daughter to her Father. I was moved to tears and felt Betty's pain as time after time she was disappointed by Bob's decisions; yet, she never faltered in her faith. What a wonderful example Betty set for her children to base their lives on standing firm on commitments made before God and never giving up.

—Pat Thomason
Author of *Mama Sewed Buttons on Its Face and I Thought That It Could See*

Before I ever met Betty face to face, I knew her through the testimonies of her children. Like the children of Israel told of God's faithfulness from generation to generation, Steve and Brenda shared how God had been so faithful to "Mrs. Jesus" (Ps. 89:1). My family, friends, and other Christ-followers are the benefactors of all Betty has sown into the hearts of her children and their children. The Smiths' kids have definitely inherited the gift of being contagious from their parents, Bob and Betty. They are easy to love, and I am so grateful for Betty's investment in her jewels and her "in-loves."

What a blessing Betty's books are to me. In Betty's first book, *Around the World in Seventy Years*, we saw how Jesus took what little she had to offer (some bread and fish) and fed the multitudes in China, Africa, Mexico, Brazil, and Powder Springs, Georgia. In *Nothing Wasted* we get an up-close and detailed view of God's handywork.

In our faith journey, there are no shortcuts, and life can be "so daily and so hard." Yet, God's provision is more than enough. Our family has been through some very dark valleys during my daughter's battle against leukemia. Part of His provision for us is Betty daily taking Communion for and praying for Katherine. In *Nothing Wasted*, we see that the enemy presented several shortcuts to Betty that appeared to be an easy way out but would have ended in a sacrifice of her intimacy with the Savior. How many times do we choose expedience over perseverance and miss the blessings God has for us?

While spending time with the Smiths, I was always overwhelmed by how gracious and forgiving Betty's approach was to Bob. What I learned from Betty is reinforced in her book: as we pray for God to perfect others and clean them up, our prayer becomes an open invitation for God to change our hearts. The more aware I am of the work God still has yet to do in me, the less critical I am of what He has yet to do in others.

If you have ever felt weary from the journey and wondered if God cares about the details, you need to read this book. Betty's story in *Nothing Wasted* is a song of redemption. In *The Message* paraphrase of the Bible, Psalm 51:13 reads, "Give me a job of teaching rebels your ways so the lost can find their way home." Betty, thank you for teaching us, and welcome home, Bob!

—David Arnold
Founder, BreakFree Ministries, Inc.
Vice President of sales
and marketing, First Acceptance Corporation

Nothing Wasted

BETTY T. SMITH

Nothing Wasted by Betty T. Smith
Published by Creation House
A Strang Company
600 Rinehart Road
Lake Mary, Florida 32746
www.strangbookgroup.com

Unless otherwise noted, all Scripture quotations are from the King James Version of the Bible.

The names of many individuals mentioned in this book have been changed to protect their identities.

Design Director: Bill Johnson
Cover design by Amanda Potter

Library of Congress Control Number: 2009926434
International Standard Book Number: 978-1-59979-772-4

First Edition

09 10 11 12 13 — 9 8 7 6 5 4 3 2 1
Printed in the United States of America

Dedication

In loving memory of
Robert Lee Smith,
my soul mate

Contents

Acknowledgments . . . ix
Introduction . . . 1
1 First Comes Love and Then Marriage . . . 3
2 Adventure in Kansas . . . 9
3 Then Comes the Baby Carriage . . . 15
4 We Are Family . . . 19
5 A Shattered World . . . 27
6 "I AM" with You . . . 37
7 First Wild West Trip . . . 45
8 The Boom Is About to Be Lowered . . . 51
9 The Dreaded Divorce . . . 57
10 Blessings from Sweden . . . 63
11 Literally Going on with Life . . . 71
12 Around the World in Seventy Years . . . 77
13 Second Wild West Trip . . . 89
14 Indian Springs . . . 103
15 Almost, but Not Quite . . . 111
16 Presenting My Case . . . 119
17 Shouting Time . . . 125
18 Letting Go and Letting God . . . 129
19 Testing Time Again! . . . 139
20 Change Is in the Air . . . 145
21 Celebration . . . 163

Acknowledgments

My heartfelt thanks extend to the team at Creation House, specifically Allen Quain, Ginny Maxwell, and Atalie Anderson, who patiently worked with me to present the most excellent work possible to my readers, and to Jill Growney, my "at home" editor and cheerleader.

I expressly address David Phelps, my mentor and mission leader, who constantly pushes me out of my comfort zone and trusts the Holy Spirit to use my availability and guard us from embarrassment. David, I follow you because you follow Jesus.

Extra special thanks to Maglean's Militia and the Prayer Force of Powder Springs First United Methodist Church, handmaidens of the Lord who practice true religion, especially every Wednesday. Dear sisters, I cherish your love and support.

Finally, dearest family of precious jewels, you light up my life and make my cup run over. Truly I am blessed among women.

Thanks, "you all"!

Introduction

MANY PEOPLE APPROACHED me after reading my first book, *Around the World in Seventy Years*, which covered short-term mission trips over the course of my life, wanting to know in more detail about my twenty-eight year marriage, briefly mentioned in the introduction of that book. They questioned, Why the breakup? How did you cope? Etcetera, etcetera. Some said there was more I needed to say, that it was evident I was still in love with my former husband, Bob. A pastor-friend urged me to tell that story, but I thought it might be boring to others; I knew it would be painful for me. Additionally, at the time of our conversation, I believed the tale was still unfolding and had no ending.

I earnestly sought the wise counsel of fellow believers I trusted and received their confirmation. As I bowed before God in prayer, in my spirit I heard Him say, "It is a story that needs to be told."

I had almost finished this book and was in the fine-tuning stage when I received a card from a dear sister-in-Christ, whom I consider to be wise indeed and very much in tune with the Holy Spirit. Her words were, "I feel in my spirit a new book on the burner—about your life." I had to laugh; I get it, Lord! The Word says, "In the multitude of counsellors there is safety" (Prov. 11:14).

And so, dear reader, here is my love story. May it encourage, edify, and exhort you. As you walk with me, I believe you will discover a God of integrity who is surprisingly economical. He keeps every promise and does not waste anything!

Chapter 1

First Comes Love and Then Marriage

Bob and I met, or should I say "bumped into each other," as he was leaving and I was entering Melvina's English class at Hapeville High School. (Hapeville is suburb of Atlanta, Georgia, located south of the airport.) Bob seemed to take joy in knocking me into the wall, and I dismissed him as some sort of jerk. That summer I received a call from Bob Smith, asking me for a date. I accepted because I thought this was another Bob, whom I knew from another school. I was surprised when the Bob Smith who came for me was the "jerk"! However, we had a super time that evening and continued dating for three years.

Bob would come to my home every Wednesday

evening after my choir practice. I was a member of the Hapeville Presbyterian Church, while he was a member of the Hapeville Methodist Church. My "muther" (nickname for my mother) would cook fried peach pies especially for him.

On Saturday nights, we went to the fabulous Fox Theater in downtown Atlanta. Everything is better at the Fox! They have a magnificent pipe organ that arises magically from the orchestra pit. The fun part is to "sing along" with the bouncing ball as it hits each note of the lyrics to the "oldies but goodies" shown on the screen. The sound fills the theater, which is decorated like a castle. There are balconies along the side walls toward the front of the auditorium, where "royalty" is seated. A parapet runs across the castle wall in the ceiling above the stage, with an open sky, floating clouds, and twinkling stars. The carpets are oriental Persian, and there are ornate chairs and sofas in the lounges and marble-topped tables.

After the movie, it was tradition to go to the Varsity, located just blocks from the Georgia Tech campus. The Varsity's famous motto is "No food over twenty-four hours old." We would park in the football area, where Flopsy, wearing a crazy hat, would sing the menu. I always ordered a chili dog, French fries (real, not frozen), P.C. (plain chocolate milk), and a fried peach pie. In those days, no one gave cholesterol a second thought.

Bob was pursuing a business administration degree through the University of Georgia, Atlanta Division, while commuting from home. He was finishing his second year at the time of my graduation from Hapeville High. I had a secret dream of going to New York City, where I would become a famous artist. However, love blossomed, and Bob did not want to wait any longer. I could not bear the thought of living my life without him, and I knew in my heart that to be his wife and the mother of his children was infinitely more important than adding another starving artist to the world. I did pray long and hard before saying yes to Bob, because it could have been me speaking to my heart instead of God. I asked Him to stop me if this marriage were not in agreement with His plan for my life.

There were only open doors, and so we married in the Hapeville Presbyterian Church on June 29, 1952, in a simple but beautiful ceremony. I especially wanted to include in my vows those words from Ruth 1:16–17:

> Intreat me not to leave thee, or to return from following after thee: for whither thou goest, I will go; and where thou lodgest, I will lodge: thy people shall be my people, and thy God my God: Where thou diest, will I die, and there will I be buried: the Lord do so to me, and more also, if ought but death part thee and me.

It was in this church at the age of thirteen that I had asked Jesus to come into my heart and experienced that "good, warm feeling" John Wesley of Methodism described. I knew then I had done a very good thing. Five years later, at the age of eighteen, I was there to officially give my heart to Bob, and I knew it, too, was a very good thing.

Muther made my wedding dress of white organdy, and my maid of honor and bridesmaids were dressed in pastel colors of organdy, like a rainbow. This was most appropriate, because the rainbow is the symbol of God's covenant with Noah (Gen. 6:48), and it also represented our marriage covenant. In later years the rainbow would prove to be a most significant sign to me of the Lord's guidance.

We began our married life in a one-room furnished apartment in our hometown of Hapeville, sharing the living room, kitchen, and bathroom with other tenants. Bob had difficulty finding an affordable place for us, and he was so proud to show me our future home. It would not have been my first choice, but it was a starting point, and we had each other. That made it perfect!

The only furniture we owned was my hope chest, which was popular with young ladies at that time. It was actually a cedar chest, which contained the sterling silver flatware with Damask Rose pattern I had purchased during the years I worked after school. We had some nice wedding gifts as well, but everything fit into the hope chest. Muther had crocheted a lovely doily, which decorated the top of the chest. To straighten the doily and the entire bedroom took me about five minutes per day, which left me with a lot of time on my hands until my wonderful husband came home from work.

Thankfully, this situation only lasted a few months, and we moved into a garage apartment in nearby East Point. The privacy was exhilarating. I had my own kitchen! I could conceive nothing better, but in another few months, we were able to swing our own little house in Forest Park (another suburb of Atlanta) with the help of Bob's father. We needed more income, so I got a job at a freight line in West End Atlanta to help with mortgage payments and

Bob's education. He was working at a loan office in downtown Atlanta and continuing evening college classes.

We attended Forest Park United Methodist Church, where Bob was treasurer, and we served with another couple as co-counselors of the youth group. I look back with mixed emotions on this experience. We had some contests and increased the attendance, as the kids were having fun, and we did have teachings; but we were young ourselves and spiritually immature. I especially remember that the other counselors, Bob, and I decided to take one Sunday off because we wanted to watch a new television show, *Maverick*. I regret that to this very day, because I failed the kids and the Lord. Sin is not all it is cracked up to be, as here I am some fifty years later still with regrets, but our God does not waste anything! I learned that we must serve with excellence at all times, and bottom line, we can trust the Lord to take up the slack. He wants our availability to be the conduit for His ability.

There is an old saying that time flies when you're having fun, and I was having fun being Bob's wife. He was always upbeat and optimistic, enjoying life to the fullest. We laughed a lot and loved a lot.

Chapter 2

Adventure in Kansas

IMMEDIATELY UPON GRADUATION from college, Bob received his orders to report to the U.S. Army, and on July 22, 1954, he left for Fort Jackson, South Carolina. After basic training, he was stationed in Fort Riley, Kansas, so we rented our house, I quit my job, and we headed west. The only other time I had left Georgia was on our honeymoon to Florida, so this was a great adventure! I had never seen so much snow in all my life, and when we made a pit stop, I was shocked that the water in the toilet was frozen. At our young age, it was just another funny incident to provoke us to laughter. We drove through the breathtaking, scenic Midwest, and when we arrived in Junction City, it, too, was blanketed in snow. Some of the streets were cordoned off so the children could play on their sleds. I was in a winter wonderland. However, some of the wonder wore off as I later had to walk to work in this slushy, cold snow. But that was later, and right then we were blessed to find a basement apartment in the home of a widow named Bertie.

We loved our little place, and Bertie was a delight. She was amazed at our banana and peanut butter sandwiches, and a pineapple sandwich blew her mind. She was lonely and wanted to spend a lot of time with us, which was fine at the beginning but called for adjustments on our part as time progressed. Sad to say, the situation became very uncomfortable for us, and we were fortunate a few months later to move into the terrace apartment of Marie and Oscar.

At our first meeting, Oscar was proudly showing us his strawberry patch. He held out a huge strawberry for Bob to admire, whereupon Bob took the strawberry from his hand and ate it! I thought to myself, "We won't get this apartment," but we did. Every Tuesday evening, we would go upstairs to watch *The Sixty-Four Thousand Dollar Question*, and Marie would serve us regular-sized Milky Way candy bars cut into little squares (this was before "miniatures"). Oscar and Marie were like surrogate parents to us, and we lived with them until it was time to go home.

The rent from our house in Georgia was paying those mortgage payments, but now we had rent to pay on our apartment, plus living expenses. Bob's income had been cut drastically, so the bottom line was that either I would have to get a job or go home, which was out of the question. In high school I had taken academic courses, but fortunately had elected shorthand and typing. The only job listed in the local paper for which I was qualified was as a secretary for Attorney Weary. I was surprised when I was granted an interview. I had practiced taking dictation from the radio, but I found that Attorney Weary talked so slowly, I could have written it in longhand. I liked this little lawyer immediately. He was in his seventies, rather short, and of a slight build. He was a man of great integrity and got right to the point. He did not hesitate to give his clients sound advice—or more like orders. When he dictated to me, he would lean back as far as he could in his wooden swivel chair and hang his legs over the side leaf of his desk, all the while cutting his fingernails with his pocket knife. I expected him to tip over at any minute, but he never did.

I was in hog heaven in my new surroundings with my husband and a job I enjoyed. We made many new friends from all over the country, and that expanded my vision. At the local U.S.O., we were Number Two seeds in ping-pong. Only one couple from California could defeat us, and we liked them very much, so that was no problem, plus it gave us a goal. There were quiz games with a limit of three correct answers per person, the prize being candy, so Bob would answer three and I would answer three. That's how we got our treats each month. Movies on base were twenty-five cents each. Life was good!

My job then became more of a challenge. Attorney Weary's son joined the practice from a big law firm in Kansas City. He talked a mile a minute and read pages from the law books when he dictated. He expected me to take down every word, but I would only write the first few words and the last few words, making sure I had the correct citation. Later I would get the cite, and transcribe it verbatim. His expectations stretched me, and I became an efficient legal secretary. You could compare the situation to that of the mama eagle who pulls the feathers out of her eaglets' nest, making it very uncomfortable and forcing them to fly. This big-city attorney helped me fly!

But that was not all! Attorney Sangster subsequently joined the firm, and I was forced to grow even more in my legal skills. He was city attorney for the adjacent small town of Manhattan. As his secretary, I learned about zoning and city ordinances. My field was becoming even more well rounded. God was not wasting anything!

Bob's tour of duty came during the Korean War, but blessedly he served the entire time as a company clerk at Fort Riley, with the exception of maneuvers on Operation Sagebrush in Louisiana, which lasted only several weeks. The only fly in the ointment during this stint was not actually a fly, but a rat. At night while lying in bed, I could hear a gnawing behind the bedroom wall, like a varmint chewing on wood. I was terrified that this monster would eat through the wall and then come to chew on me. I told Oscar, but he dismissed me as being paranoid because Bob was gone. He did look around, but found no evidence, until one day he heard the noise, too. Then he put out bait, and the creature supposedly got so thirsty that he ran away looking for water and died—far, far away, perhaps in neighboring Missouri! I was ecstatic when my husband/protector came home.

Looking back, which is always 20/20, I wish I had enjoyed that tour of duty more than I actually did. I was homesick and missed my family, so I was glad for the early release. I wanted to get back to our house and start our family. After all, we had been married four years.

Chapter 3

Then Comes the Baby Carriage

HAVING BABIES PROVED to be easier said than done because I had endometriosis. The doctor recommended several procedures, including hormone shots and x-ray treatments. After almost a year, I told the doctor I wanted to take the summer off, and he said it would not make any difference at all, that he would perform surgery in the fall. I worked for a law firm in downtown Atlanta, a very good job that I received based on all that experience in Kansas.

As I walked back to the office from my lunch break, I gazed at the historic clock at the Five Points intersection, and spoke to the Lord, "If You want me to have surgery to prove to You how much I want a baby, I will, but from this moment on, I will not worry about it." And I didn't. Bob and I agreed we would adopt if we were not pregnant by the first of the year.

We had moved from our first little house in Forest Park to a larger home with a basement just a few miles away in a new subdivision. Workmen had left granite slabs alongside our road. Bob decided to use one for a step onto our patio, so we took our little red cart down the hill and loaded the slab onto it. When the wheels buckled on the cart, we should have heeded the warning, but we were excited about our project. The plan was to lift the slab off the cart, and then Bob would walk it over to its resting place and drop it. As I tried to lift, I lost my grip and Bob's hand was badly scraped. I felt terribly guilty, so I suggested we try again. This time I strained with all my might. Apparently I fainted, because the next thing I knew, I was lying on the bed and Bob was slapping me with a cold, wet washcloth, crying, "Please don't die, please don't die!"

The diagnosis was a sprained back, but God was not wasting anything! That October I conceived, and the following April 17, 1959, our son Steve was born. My grandmother said it was because when I lifted the slab, all my female organs were put in the right place!

I had promised God that if He would give me a son, I would give him a Bible name, so we named him Steven Lee. Stephen was the first Christian martyr (Acts 6–7), and Lee was the middle name of Bob's mother. In later years I repented that I had spelled Steve with a *v* instead of *ph*, but the Lord assured me I had not made a mistake because the *v* was for victory! When Steve is on the scene,

I know everything will be just fine. He has an assurance about him, and he reminds me of pure, shining gold.

My Papa Carson (Muther's father) had died the year before, and he passed with the concern on his heart that I was barren and facing surgery. I believe that when he got to heaven, he marched up to that throne of grace and had a little talk with Jesus, because the following year Steve was born just three days prior to Papa Carson's birthday, and there was no surgery!

It did not occur to me that we would have more children. I was content with my "prayer baby." When I discovered I was pregnant again, I was shocked. What a wonderful surprise!

Lamar Scott came into the world with a bang, which was indicative of his life to come. I was in the shower when my water broke. Fortunately, Steve was with his Grandmother Hattie. We made a mad dash to the hospital with the gas gauge on empty. Bob had one hand on the wheel, and he was reaching out to me on the back seat with his other hand, wanting so much to help. I could feel Scott's head crowning, and I was desperately trying to hold him in with a towel. We came into the emergency area the wrong way down a one-way street. Bob grabbed a nurse coming out of the cafeteria, snatched her tray, and yelled, "My wife is having a baby!"

In seconds, I was in a wheelchair, bursting through double doors (like in the movies). In the maternity ward the doctor asked how far apart my pains were, to which I replied, "One on top of the other!" He looked, agreed, and rushed me into delivery.

Scott was born on May 17, 1964, before Bob had time to call the family. He was named Lamar after Bob's father, and Scott because it suited him, plus we wanted his name to start with an *s*. He is an artist, creative and sensitive, and in that world he is known as Lamar, while to family and friends he is Scott. He is bull-headed, not easily moved, but loyal and compassionate. He hates injustice!

Bob and I moved temporarily to the Pensacola, Florida, area so he could obtain sales experience with his employer, a paint company, with the goal of becoming their credit manager. His family came for a visit, but I did not feel well while they were there. Shortly thereafter I was elated to learn I was again pregnant. I asked the Lord that if it would not make a big difference in His scheme of things, could I please have a girl? And He obliged.

We lived in Gulf Breeze, across the bay from Pensacola. Because of my delivery history with Scott, the doctor insisted on induced labor. It was convenient to have a baby by appointment, on November 8, 1965, but not as exciting as dashing down one-way streets the wrong way on empty; however, I was more than willing to forego that kind of excitement. We named our little daughter Stacey Elizabeth. Stacey met the requirements of the *s*, and Elizabeth was Muther's name. Stacey is an amazing elementary school teacher, choir director, and worship leader who adores Jesus. She is like a bottle of cola, fizzing and effervescent.

So much for endometriosis. I had been healed!

Chapter 4

We Are Family

To my mind, our time in Florida was comparable to Kansas. I considered it a tour of duty because I was homesick. I wanted my children to be near their grandparents. Additionally, I could not find my place in our neighborhood; I had no friends. The clique seemed impenetrable. As a mother of three—a newborn, a toddler, and a kindergartner—I was extremely busy just keeping up with them and the house. We lived across the street from the canal that led into Santa Rosa Sound, our house backed up to a golf course that was under construction, and we were just a few miles from the Gulf and Pensacola Beach. I would have enjoyed it more had I known our stay would be brief and had I known what lay in store back in Georgia.

Steve, though only five, was a fisherman, and he loved going over to the canal to fish from the neighbor's dock. He also enjoyed the golf course, playing on the sand dunes. One day, he came screaming to the back door. I opened it to see him with a horny toad latched onto his bare little midriff. I reached out to grab it but just could not put my hands on that monster. Then his friend, our neighbor's little girl, bravely removed it. I rushed him to the clinic to get a tetanus shot, filled with guilt because of my cowardice. Some kind of mother I was!

We went through two hurricanes during our sixteen-month stay in Florida. Both times Bob was in Atlanta on company business, so it was my responsibility to tape up the windows, fill the bathtubs with water spiced with a little bleach, have the grill ready, and stock up on the appropriate groceries. Steve came to my bed one night during a storm asking me to stop the jet planes from flying outside his window so he could sleep! It was laughable to me that the only high ground was on the hill where the Baptist church stood. There was a message in there somewhere!

Our home had terrazzo floors, and the living room, dining area, and kitchen were one large open space. Scott had a child's walker with wheels, and he would tear across those floors, cutting corners on two wheels. He had a playpen, but he would never play in it; so we stored his toys there. The only place to keep something out of his reach was the top of the refrigerator. Toilet training was a joke, as he was really too young and not the least bit interested. He just wore the plastic potty on top of his head, like a helmet.

Stacey was my sweet baby girl, so far just nursing,

sleeping, and cooing. If I had been more blessed, there would have to have been two of me! Still, I longed for home.

When Bob saw that his dream of becoming credit manager was not to be, he decided the following spring to return to Georgia. We purchased a new home in College Park, close to the Atlanta airport. Bob began working for a clothing manufacturing company in their credit department. Steve was enrolled in the first grade, and Bob kindly fenced in the backyard in an attempt to restrain Scott, especially during the times I was nursing Stacey.

Steve had a good friend named Paul, and one day they gathered over twenty-five turtles and corralled them within our fence. They (the turtles, that is) became a bit odoriferous over time, and it was a happy day when the boys set them free.

Scott also had a friend named Sarah, whom he called "Sadra." She lived with her family to the rear of us on a cul-de-sac. Scott would climb to the top of our fence and fall over, always tearing his pants, to get to Sadra. One day, they set fire to our side neighbor's front yard and attempted to extinguish the flames with a Coke bottle filled with water. Another day, the two of them decided to take a little stroll, and the whole neighborhood was disbursed to rescue them. They were found, innocently walking hand-in-hand just a few blocks away.

Several years later, we decided to buy some land and build our dream home. We discovered five acres a few miles south in the Fairburn area. Bob's parents were being forced to leave their home in Hapeville because of the expansion of the Atlanta airport, so we divided the land. They took two acres fronting on the highway, and we took three acres fronting on Peters Road. We had a "compound," with a path between our houses.

Our property had a small pond; the neighbors to the rear of our house had a lake; and the neighbors on the other side had a swimming pool, tennis court, and a mule the kids could ride. Bob's parents had a basketball court and a curving driveway with a hill, which was perfect for skateboards and Big Wheels. It was an ideal situation for active youngsters. We had land to clear, and my cup was running over (Ps. 23:5). We hauled in rocks from our property and the local quarry to build a wall. It was fun to see the children with their wheelbarrows working like little farmhands. We marked their growth on the kitchen doorframe. They were thriving, doing well in school, active in sports, and involved in St. Andrew United Methodist Church.

But a storm was looming over the horizon, not yet seen or felt. Her name was Debbie, our goddaughter. Her parents were going through a divorce in Missouri and asked if Debbie could live with us until her mother could reestablish a home back in Georgia. We were delighted to have Debbie but sad about the circumstances. Her father, Dick, had gone to school with Bob, and Liz, her mother, was my dearest friend. We played cards together on Saturday nights, went on family vacations, and had our babies almost simultaneously. When Debbie came, she turned my world upside down. My perfect little family was in chaos. Debbie shared a room with Stacey, and she would wake up screaming from nightmares, dreaming her father was chasing her with a knife. This was a tumultuous time for her, with parents on the verge of divorce, separated from her brothers, and a new school environment surrounded by strangers. We kept loving her, trying to make her a part of our family, and in a short time the nightmares ended. Stacey was a real trooper, and Debbie was blessed to have her as a roommate in spite of the difference in age.

Debbie did not take school seriously, and her choice of friends was questionable, to say the least. I asked God to protect us from any mistakes, and He was faithful. For instance, Debbie was to attend a party, but her friends failed to come for her. We didn't find out until after the fact that it was a pot party. We also learned that Debbie had been skipping school.

Bob said we should just coast along and keep the peace since she would be leaving soon. He did not think a confrontation would change the situation. But this was Debbie, and her life mattered—she mattered to me and to God—so I talked with her from my heart, as mother to daughter. Her response was one of agitation, because her conscience was being awakened. She said that before she came to us things did not make a difference, but now they did; and she was asking what I had done to her. It certainly was not me, but the Holy Spirit. I wish I could say that Debbie accepted Christ as we talked. She did not, however, and I felt that I was a failure. I was at wit's end (Ps. 107:27).

Our church was holding a mini-revival the last weekend in May 1975, and on that Saturday night I went to the altar. I cried out, "Lord, I cannot cope. If You are real, show me, or I'm getting out of your church." He accepted the challenge. My life passed in front of my eyes, like a drowning man. God spoke to my spirit, "When in your life have things not worked out for you?"

Then the Holy Spirit filled me, starting at my toes and going up my body to the top of my head, like a thermometer. I knew He was real, and He loved me! It was like getting new glasses when you don't realize you need them. You see so clearly. My world had been washed, shiny and clean.

When I returned home, Bob and the kids were on the floor watching television. Later they went to bed, and I waited for Debbie to return from her date. I had picked up a book at church entitled *On Tiptoe with Joy* by John T. Seamands, which dealt with the baptism of the Holy Spirit. The disciples were not drunk as the people claimed, but they had received that which the Prophet Joel had prophesied; they had been filled with the Holy Spirit (Joel 2:28–29). I knew absolutely nothing about this phenomenon, but I knew one thing for sure: it had happened to me, and it was authentic. My life took on a new dimension, a new power with a hunger for God's Word, and a longing to serve Him.

The following morning, Bob said to me, "You got religion last night, didn't you?" I was surprised. How did he know? I had not said a word.

Then I replied, "Yes, let me tell you about it." I described what had happened to me, and his response was, "That's nice." I knew then in my heart of hearts that my husband did not know the Lord. He knew about Him, but it was not personal. There was no relationship.

Debbie left a few months later to live with her mother. I owe her a debt of gratitude. God used her to show me more of Himself; He did not waste anything! In just a few years, I would need as much of God as I could hold.

Debbie today works with hurting women. It takes one to know one, and she is excellent in her field. I still pray for that day when she discovers for herself the reality of Jesus and is at last free from the bondage of depression.

Chapter 5

A Shattered World

Franklin Roosevelt described December 7, 1941, as a day of infamy. My year of infamy was 1978. It started the first week of January, when my dad was diagnosed with terminal cancer. He made Muther promise she would not tell my sister and me the extent of his illness, but I am so glad she did.

When I was alone with him, I told him I knew. "What do you think you know?" he asked. I replied that I knew the seriousness of his condition, but there was another thing I needed to know, "How are you with the Lord?" Then he sat straight up in bed, and emphatically said, "Jesus Christ is my Savior; He always has been and He always will be!"

That satisfied me, and I told him that I would meet him

one day at the middle gate of the south wall. Meanwhile, he did not have to worry about Muther; I would take care of her, and she would never be put into a nursing home. That was the last lucid conversation I had with my father.

My dad was not a talkative man, and I cannot remember a time when he said he loved me. However, he showed his love by his hard work providing for Muther, my younger sister, and me. He demonstrated his love for his nation by enlisting in the U.S. Marine Corps during World War II. We did not see him for three years. He wrote from Iwo Jima, saying that the Movietone newsmen were there filming and for us to look for him sitting on top of a tank. He would be wearing a black skullcap. We went to the movies every time the picture changed for a month, hoping for a glimpse of him in the war reports, to no avail.

My maternal grandmother would buy Capitola brand flour in printed cotton sacks. She would use the sacks to make towels and gave our family the tokens that came in the sacks. You could get into the movie with a token and nine cents. If I could scrounge up fifteen cents, I would have enough to get a bag of popcorn and a penny piece of candy. That was how we could afford the movies.

The next time I saw my dad was just prior to his discharge from the service. He had a layover in Atlanta on his way to Camp LeJeune, North Carolina. I was alone in my grandparents' living room, where I would go after school to listen to *The Lone Ranger* on their radio. I was a member of the Lone Ranger Safety Club and proud of my certificate of membership and silver badge. I was in my usual place on the sofa, stringing popcorn for our Christmas tree when he entered. I ran and wrapped my arms around his waist, not wanting to let go.

It was many years later that I spoke to him about the cancer, and I still did not want to let him go. I was on my way home from the hospital when my Lord asked me a very pointed question: "Do you think where I am is a lovely place?"

I replied, "Oh, yes!"

He continued, "Then why do you not want your dad to be here with Me?" I released my dad.

I had just arrived home when the phone rang. It was my sister, urging me to return to the hospital. I drove down the street that night, and as I made the turn onto another street at the bottom of the hill, I had a vision. My dad was walking with Jesus down a grassy path, lined with trees and green shrubbery. He was dressed in his regular pants and shirt, while Jesus wore a white robe. My eyes zeroed in, and I was so happy to see they were holding hands. I sensed that Jesus was taking my dad home; there was a peace that was tangible. There could be no sadness here, because my dad was free, well, safe, and loved beyond all measure.

This was a treasured gift to me, so tender from the heart of my heavenly Father. When I reached the hospital and held Muther in my arms, I relayed the vision to her in detail. This brought her comfort that was sorely needed. There is an enormity to the grief one experiences in the loss of a mate. They were both eighteen when they married, and had been together forty-four years. It's like losing the other half of yourself.

My eldest son, Steve, was unable to attend the funeral

because approximately one week earlier he had been involved in a serious accident. His car had stalled alongside the road during a rainstorm. That evening, he and his friend Herbert drove over to jump-start it. Herbert's car was facing Steve's car, so they could connect the battery cables. Both of them were standing between the two cars when another car ran off the road, hitting Herbert's car in the rear and pinning the boys' legs. We got that call that parents dread: "Your son has been involved in an accident."

Herbert had a broken leg, while Steve had crushed calf muscles in his left leg. Even today, that muscle does not extend properly down his leg, and he walks on his toes; however, the weight of shoes helps bring the foot down, and the limp is not noticeable unless he is barefoot. He says he can tell when the weather is going to change.

As an aside, in later years Herbert fell from a tree and was paralyzed from his neck down. I have never met a more courageous young man, with a more loving wife and family. He has been a faithful friend to my son, and they have worked for many years for the same company. It makes you wonder if God allows these minor tragedies to strengthen us for the bigger stuff down the road.

Along these same lines, while driving Steve to a doctor's appointment concerning his leg, I made the comment that I felt something else was coming. This was not all, and the next thing would be big. I was right!

Bob wanted to take our family vacation the first part of June, but I wanted to delay a bit so we would be gone Father's Day weekend because of my dad's passing. I thought I could handle the grief better if I were away from home. However, Bob prevailed, so off we went to Panama City, Florida.

We spent a lot of time on the beach, playing volleyball and flying kites. Other families challenged us in volleyball, but we Smiths were undefeated! One afternoon, I was sitting by the pool, reading a book, when Bob approached. He wanted to take me to the store so I could choose a birthday present.

I smiled and said, "I have everything I want—we're a family." Then he turned and walked away, and I returned to my book.

Bob had his own business at this time, a manufacturing company called Estex. In earlier years, when Steve was just a baby, we had a couple of coin-op laundries, but he later sold those for a good profit. Bob was an astute businessman. Wayne, our brother-in-law, said he was like a cat. You could throw him up in the air, and he would always land on his feet.

After the laundries, Bob purchased a dry cleaners in our hometown of Hapeville. We privately called it our "laughing place." This was because all we had was invested in it when polyester made its debut, striking a mortal blow to our business. It was enough to make us cry, but we chose to laugh instead. My salary at a downtown law firm was paying the wages of our other two employees. Our grocery money came from Bob's winnings at poker from the guys at the used car lot next door.

Bob did not like failure and was even more determined that Estex would be a success. He wore all the caps, from manager to salesman to janitor. Even our children helped

(Scott called it "slave labor"), and for one order, I made yarn tassels for some horse blankets. We were giving it our best shot.

Shortly after our vacation ended, Bob went to South Carolina on a sales trip. He called and was crying, saying that he had hurt me. I had been praying for his salvation, so I thought the Holy Spirit was drawing him. I said that while it did hurt that he would not go to church with us, or go to hear Steve sing, all he had to do was get on his knees and surrender his life to Jesus. He didn't go into any more detail and said he would see me the next day, which would be Sunday. I was excited, because I thought he would come home a changed man. I asked Steve to pray and also called his twin sister, Barbara, who had been my prayer partner for her brother's conversion.

I could hardly wait for church to be over the next day, but a funny thing happened on the way to my purported victory. As we were in the parking lot, I stared at the back of a friend's striped T-shirt, and the thought came, "He wants a divorce." I dismissed that as ridiculous, straight from the pit of hell.

Bob did come home, but not light-hearted and gay; he was heavy-hearted and sad, carrying the weight of the world on his shoulders. Steve perceived the situation, and immediately took Scott and Stacey next door to swim.

Bob sat in a chair in the living room, and as I knelt at his feet, he confessed to me that he had been having an affair for ten years with Maxine. This was my "friend" who had previously worked with him at another job. He had even asked my permission to employ her at Estex! The whole episode was surreal.

As he spoke, I could feel the wind, the waves, and the water coming over me (Luke 6:48), but I knew I would not go under. I told him that he had a decision to make, that we could go for counseling, but he said he had to get off by himself and think. I begged him not to go; however, he walked out the door, leaving my heart shredded into a million pieces.

People say you always know when your mate is cheating, but I disagree. We didn't fuss or fight, and my husband had even told me the night before he left on his last trip that he truly loved me. When I asked him about that later, he replied that he didn't even know what love was. How sad. I did, and he was the one with the college degree.

That brings to mind Forrest Gump, from the movie of the same name. He was mentally challenged and deeply in love with Jennie. He told her that while he was "not a smart man," he knew what love was. I was not mentally challenged, but I was emotionally challenged, and I loved my husband, regardless. I felt pity for him, because when you don't have the power of the Holy Spirit in you and working for you, it is extremely difficult to resist the enemy's tactics. He is in the business of destroying families, and Bob fell into the trap.

The only bright spot I could see at this time was that my son Steve was relieved of a mighty burden. I had asked him numerous times if something were wrong, but he would never tell me; now he did. Someone at school had told him of his dad's affair, and he had even staked out across the street from Maxine's house to see if it were true. He had kept that information from me for two years, and at last told our pastor, who counseled him to tell me. I took that heavy load from my son and told him I would carry it now. How blessed I was and still am today to have this son of my love, who continually seeks to shield and protect me!

After Bob drove away that earth-shattering afternoon, I went on our deck to sit and pray. The Lord reminded me of "that time in the plane," and I immediately knew what He meant. Several months after Stacey's birth, Bob had taken me on a surprise trip to California, even arranging for a babysitter. When we departed Atlanta, the skies were cloudy and gray, but when we climbed above the clouds, the sun was shining, turning them into a brilliant gold. I thought, "This must be what the streets of heaven are like!"

I kept that scene to myself and would think of it from time to time—just something special between my Lord and me—and now He was bringing it to my remembrance. He said, "I will be your Son-light. I will walk with you through this, and when you get to the other side, you will have a good marriage. Come, walk with me and be My love; the best is yet to be."

Well, hallelujah! All I had to do was keep my faith, walk with my Lord, and one day Bob would come home. My marriage would be restored. I did not realize then that I was in for a very long, slow walk. In Psalm 23, He promises to be our Shepherd and to walk with us through the valley. I wanted to run and get it over quickly; also, I was not too thrilled about the "through" part, either. Couldn't we just skip or hop or jump over, and cut out all that middle part? No, the Lord had more in mind.

One thing I knew for certain, and that was that I must forgive Bob. It was not just for his sake, but also for mine. I had to remain in strict obedience to God to keep the channel wide open between us. He commands, not suggests, that we forgive others, and He gave us the example by forgiving those who crucified Him as He hung on the cross (Luke 23:34). In the Lord's Prayer, He says that we are forgiven in the same manner that we forgive others (Matt. 6:12).

Forgiveness is not a one-step operation, it is a process, and I began by prostrating myself on my bedroom floor, crying out to the Lord to forgive Bob through me and to remove any bitterness. I felt His cleansing touch as I lay on that floor with my face in the carpet. I was free, and I knew Bob was released from any chains of unforgiveness on my part. There would be occasions in the coming years when I would confirm aloud, "I forgive," but it was first done in my spirit there on my bedroom floor.

The first time Bob came to take the kids out after he left was to an Atlanta Braves ball game. They were excited, and as they piled into the car, they said, "Come on, Mom. Go with us."

I smiled and shook my head; I was not invited. I encouraged them to have a great time, and I went inside for a good cry.

The first Christmas without Bob was crushing for me. I stayed up on Christmas Eve into the wee hours of the morning, attempting to assemble a table hockey game for the boys. The main problem was, I did not know what a Phillip's head screwdriver was, or even if I had one. I caved in under the pressure, feeling so inadequate, failing again. I put the game under the tree "as is." To my happy surprise, the boys had more fun assembling it than playing the game!

When we get bumped, we spill what we are full of, and I wanted to spill the fruit of the Spirit, which is love, joy, peace, patience, kindness, gentleness, goodness, faith, and self-control (Gal. 5:22). Unforgiveness and bitterness contaminate the fruit of the Spirit. It would take the power of the Holy Spirit to bring forth that fruit in me, especially that "patience" one, but I could count on His faithfulness as long as I remained yielded.

I asked myself these questions: Would my husband want to return home to a mean-spirited, bitter woman? Would that be a true reflection of my Lord? I thought not!

Chapter 6

"I AM" with You

I WAS BLESSED TO have a special group of prayer warriors at St. Andrew United Methodist Church, and I learned the importance of the body of Christ. We are not Lone Rangers on this battlefield of life. It is critical that we lock together our shields of faith to form an impenetrable wall of protection. The Bible admonishes us not to forsake "the assembling of ourselves together" (Heb. 10:25). How tempted we are when times are tough to retreat into our own little shells, but that is the enemy's scheme. We are vulnerable when we are alone. That is why the Hebrew children blew the trumpet in the wilderness during the Exodus before they broke camp (Num. 10:1–9). No one was to be left behind.

During the prayer time at one of our meetings, my friend Billy said that he saw a little yellow flower, but did not know what it meant. Then Rick, a younger friend, said he saw Jesus, and He was a Shepherd. We concluded our prayers, and Gwen, Billy's wife, said there was a book I should read entitled *Hinds' Feet on High Places* by Hannah Hurnard. I exclaimed, "I have that book at home!" It had been given to me many years earlier by a friend, but I just could not get into it, so had put it on the shelf.

When I started reading, Jesus was portrayed as the Chief Shepherd, and there was a scene wherein the main character, little Much-Afraid, as she is following the Shepherd to the high places by a very circuitous route, comes upon a little yellow flower. The name of the plant is "Acceptance-with-Joy." I have subsequently read this book at least five times, and I know the Lord gave it to me as a guidebook. He put it into my hands years before I would need it, so when I did need it, it was there. None of this was taking Him by surprise, and He was making it as easy for me as possible. Here is that "nothing wasted" principle at work again!

I asked myself this question: What do I believe that cannot be shaken? And I said aloud the Apostle's Creed that I had memorized from the Methodist hymnal:

> I believe in God, the Father Almighty, Maker of Heaven and Earth, and in Jesus Christ, His only Son, our Lord, Who was conceived by the Holy Spirit, born of the Virgin Mary, suffered under Pontius Pilate, was crucified, dead and buried. The third day He arose from the dead, He descended into Hell, He ascended into Heaven, from whence

> He shall come to judge the quick and the dead. I believe in the Holy Spirit, the holy catholic church, the communion of saints, the forgiveness of sin, the resurrection of the body, and life everlasting. World without end. Amen!

My main guidebook continued to be the Bible, and one day in my reading, I had a bright idea. Since Esther fasted for five days to save a nation, I would fast five days to save one person, Bob. And so I did, fast, that is, for five days. At the end of the fifth day, I was wondering what the Lord had been trying to teach me. I was at the end of the fast with no definite word, but as I prayed, He led me to Lamentations 3:21–26:

> This I recall to my mind, therefore I have hope. It is of the Lord's mercies that we are not consumed, because His compassions fail not. They are new every morning; great is thy faithfulness. The Lord is my portion, Saith my soul; therefore will I hope in Him. The Lord is good unto them that wait for him, to the soul that seeketh him. It is good that a man should both hope and quietly wait for the salvation of the Lord.

The "acceptance with joy" and "hoping and quietly waiting" seemed compatible but easier said than done. The waiting part is more than just a time thing. It involves serving, like waiting on tables or waiting on customers. I was not just to sit and fold my arms, waiting for God to keep His promises. I was to work in His kingdom, be about my Father's business, and as I worked and went about doing good for Him, like Jesus (Acts 11:38), He would work good for me (Rom. 8:28). I had it in my head and in my heart; but there was still the walking it out, and the enemy loves to discourage. I saw on a church bulletin board: "The Lord promises a safe arrival, but not a calm passage."

Shortly after Bob left to do his thinking, my friend Suzanne, who worked with me at the Sparrow law firm, returned from lunch with a gift for me. She had been at a local Christian bookstore when a clerk approached her with a small cedar block of wood, on which were a copper butterfly and a tiny blue plastic square, representing a page from a book. On the page were the words, "God is perfecting that thing that concerned me" (Ps. 138:8). The clerk instructed her to give it to her friend who was going through a very difficult time. Suzanne knew it was for me. I was thrilled, because this was God's promise to me that He was "perfecting" Bob, that he would be saved and come home!

I showed the gift to Muther, and she said the clerk was an angel. I repeated this to Suzanne, and she went back to the store to find the clerk; however, he was not there. She told her story to the manager, and upon describing the clerk, the manager said they had never had anyone with that description working for them. She offered to pay for the gift, but the manager emphatically declined, saying, "Oh, no! This was from God!"

That same day I received an encouraging card in the mail from a couple in our church. At the bottom of the verse Helen had written the quote from Psalm 138:8 that was on my special gift. The same message twice in one day!

I had a new hope now, a fresh word from the Lord. But

nothing changed; daily life was so hard. I slowly came to realize that God was not perfecting my husband but me. I was being led into a higher plane, a greater maturity. My Lord was cutting away those parts that were not Christlike, that Christ would not like in me. We cannot be responsible for another person's walk; their free will cannot be violated. This was *my* test, to build *my* testimony. I could intercede for Bob, but I was not the Holy Spirit.

One morning I had just pulled into my office parking lot when I had another word from God. He impressed on my heart that Psalm 126 was for me and Psalm 128 was for Bob. Psalm 126 speaks of "turning the captivity," and says, "He that goes forth weeping, bearing precious seed, shall doubtless come again with rejoicing, bringing his sheaves with him." Psalm 128 states, "Your wife shall be as a fruitful vine by the sides of your house: your children like olive plants around your table."

When Bob came over a few days later to discuss our situation, I shared these two psalms with him. While I could see God speaking to us from His Word, promising His blessings, Bob was not the least interested. He had his own agenda, and it did not include me. I was extremely frustrated, and when I was alone, I shook my fist at the sky, and cried, "Lord, don't You see what's happening? Why don't You do something about this?" In His mercy, grace, and great patience, He spoke not, but let His little girl vent. I did repent!

Psalm 91 was a great source of comfort to me, and I even committed it to memory. Verse 10 says, "There shall no evil befall thee, neither shall any plague come nigh your dwelling." Many times that verse would seem to override my prayers, as if the Lord were interrupting me. I equated divorce with an evil plague, so I interpreted this to mean I would not be divorced.

One evening while cooking supper, I cried out to God, asking Him to give me something from His Word. My heart was hurting and I needed help. I turned the pages of my Bible while I stood beside the stove, making sure our supper did not burn. I flipped over to Isaiah 54 and read from verse 4 to the end of the chapter. The Lord promised He would be my husband, that I was "a woman forsaken and grieved in spirit, and a wife of youth, when I was refused," and His promise to me was as sure as His covenant with Noah. The sign of that covenant was the rainbow, so I asked the Lord to give me a rainbow as confirmation that He was truly speaking to me.

The next day it rained, so I was looking for my rainbow. I had my hair permed, changing my former casual style to curly in an effort to transform my image. When I exited the beauty shop, the sun was shining, and there was no rainbow. Satan was whispering in my ear, "You made it all up!"

I returned home, walked into the kitchen, and to my amazement, the counter where the kids did their homework was completely cleared, and in the middle of the counter was the July 1979 *National Geographic* magazine, with a picture of Bridal Falls, Yosemite National Park. A rainbow stretched across the bottom of the falls! Our Lord is so sweet and clever.

In Isaiah 54, verse 11, God also promised me sapphires. I asked if He had looked around our house. The stove had only two burners working and no oven, the dishwasher was broken, along with the washer and dryer, the hot water heater had burst, the bathroom floor was rotten, the roof leaked, my car had a cracked block, and to top it all—there were termites! However, one by one items were repaired or replaced, and in May 1980, on Mother's Day, my children, in that very kitchen, presented me with an opal ring (rainbow stone) surrounded with tiny sapphires. They said when they were shopping in the store, they knew this was the one. I showed them Isaiah 54. They were correct—this was the one! What made this ring even more special was that they worked to pay for it, Steve with United Parcel Service (UPS), Scott at Gyro Wrap Sandwich Shop, and Stacey at the Chocolate Chip Cookie Company. Also, Brenda, Steve's future wife, was a party to the decision. Bob was missing such a blessing—his family.

Chapter 7

First Wild West Trip

Bob never did like camping, so this was a good opportunity for us to make a trip out west before he came home. I really wanted to see those Bridal Falls in Yosemite. He had been gone one year, so I was expecting him to return at any moment; I did not realize there was plenty of time. I had a red Ford station wagon, and we packed every available inch, including camping gear and a camp stove on top. Stacey had to sit on top of luggage on the back seat, beside Scott and me. Steve was our main driver, and Brenda was in the passenger seat beside him.

Bob offered to help finance the trip, but I declined. I didn't want his money; I wanted him to go with us. Since our funds were limited, the plan was to camp along the way to save lodging costs. However, we had an adventure in Two Guns, Arizona, and I had to have a bed that night. The car began to run hot, and steam was bursting forth. We pulled into a gas station where Steve and the mechanic attempted to solve the problem. They could not reach a conclusion, so I went outside and prayed, asking God for guidance. I seemed to hear, "Flush out the radiator and add anti-coolant."

I told Steve the Lord said to "drain the radiator and add anti-freeze." (I am not a car person, so I confused the language.) The attendant said we could flush the radiator and add anti-coolant, but when he did, the water was still very hot. Steve just looked at me, and I confirmed that was what I heard. So they waited a few minutes, and then the water cooled. The attendant gave us a gallon jug of water, told us just to add water from time to time, and we could finish our trip and make it safely home. I was so relieved because repairs would have taken all our money, and that would have been the end of our trip.

From Arizona we proceeded to the Grand Canyon. Steve approached me after we parked at the rim, saying he had something to show me. He took me to the edge of the canyon, and as I looked over, I had to catch my breath. I read once, "Life is not measured by the number of moments that we breathe, but the number of moments that take our breath away." This was one of those moments.

We hiked down into the canyon, awed by the stark beauty, the colors, and rock formations. The sunlight constantly changed the scenes, like a slow-moving slide show. You just had to drink it in, and we did.

We drove down to Hoover Dam and stopped in Las

Vegas. I was the only one old enough to gamble, but at the Stardust we went to the rear and I gave the kids dimes to play in the slot machines. Scott hit a jackpot and went wild! He put all his dimes in a tube sock, $10.20 in all. He said he would never spend it, but never is a very long time.

We stayed in a motel in Las Vegas, and Scott wanted to call his dad. I missed him, too, but I would not be able to restrain the tears if I had to speak. I just stayed outside while they told their dad about their adventures thus far. I missed Bob so much I could taste it.

We headed on to Yosemite along a road full of dips. There were road signs warning us of the dips, but Steve thought it was fun to jostle our bones and hit our heads on the ceiling of the car. Actually, Scott later said his favorite part of the trip was the "dips and dimes." We found a campsite and settled in amidst the scenic grandeur of Yosemite. "Scenic grandeur" is a gross understatement. If you love nature, this is heaven. The kids hiked, rode bikes and horses, swam, and tried one day to outrun a swarm of mosquitoes in one of the valleys.

I was sitting at a picnic table waiting for them one afternoon, looking up at the majestic mountains, when God reminded me, "I'm bigger than any of your problems." He indeed was my Rock and my Fortress (2 Sam. 22:2).

We did see Bridal Falls, and I took pictures. There was even a rainbow at the base of the falls, just like in the *National Geographic*! I didn't share my secret with the kids; it was between my Lord and me.

One evening we were late leaving the park to return to our campsite, and we gave a ride to two campers. They had been on the trail a long time and were a bit ripe, to put it kindly. We were glad to bid them a fond farewell. The camp store had closed, and we had to stop for supper at a local restaurant, which was very crowded. Scott and Stacey decided to walk on to the camp. Scott was admonished not to leave his sister, but he did. Rangers tried to give her a ride, but she refused to get in the car with strangers! Because Scott was miserable with poison ivy in some sensitive areas, I took pity on him and did not lower the boom.

As we departed Yosemite, Steve was driving too fast, I thought, down those mountains. When I protested, he simply stopped the car, and he and Brenda got in the back seat, while I took over the driving with Scott by my side. He and I both share a fear of heights. My stomach was in knots, my hands were sweating, and my eyes were full of tears. Scott put his hand on my knee and smiled. He knew. As I came down the pass, I saw a deer drinking in the shallows of a lake. I was praying under my breath, and then the Lord whispered to my spirit, "I do not want you to be afraid of anything I have made."

Of course, He had made it all for my pleasure. The fear did not come from Him, but from the enemy, so I was not required to receive it. His peace came, and before I knew it, we had reached the main highway and flat country again. Steve volunteered to take the wheel. As we exchanged places, I confidently said, "I could drive all the way home." And he nodded in agreement.

We stopped for lunch in a barren stretch of land, just sand and cactus, and were spreading our food on the picnic table. It seemed funny to me that this little spot was here in the middle of nowhere, an oasis for weary travelers. The table was not far from the highway, and Brenda, dressed in shorts and a T-shirt, was bending over to get drinks out of the cooler with her rear to the road. An eighteen-wheeler came barreling by, and the driver blew his air horn. Brenda about jumped out of her skin, and we were all howling with laughter.

We stopped at Oral Roberts University in Tulsa, Oklahoma, and camped in a site near the school. When we awoke the following morning, we were surrounded by rabbits. I never equated Oklahoma with rabbits, but it made for the fun start of our day.

It was grand seeing our United States, from Georgia to California, and back again: the big sky country, the mountains, and the prairies, the lakes and rivers and waterfalls, and that grand, Grand Canyon. It was the trip of a lifetime with my kids, totally awesome, and I even had one hundred dollars in my pocket when we pulled into our driveway—enough to buy a water pump for our faithful car. She deserved it!

I was not glad to be home, though. I did want to deliver Brenda safely to her parents, and there was family waiting, but not our whole family. Bob was still missing, and it was so tempting to ride off into the sunset.

Chapter 8

The Boom Is About to Be Lowered

It was almost another year before Bob filed for divorce. All this time I had been expecting him to come knocking on the door, saying he had come to his senses. Instead, it was the Fulton County marshal who came to serve the divorce complaint. I burst into tears and felt so sorry for this public servant, who also felt sorry for my family and me but had to do his duty. Divorce hurts so many people. It's no wonder that the Lord hates it and considers it an act of violence (Mal. 2:16). You can compare it to a tornado ripping through a home. Divorce rips through hearts and destroys families.

This was a bumpy patch of road for me. One evening I had driven Scott to soccer practice, and while waiting for him to finish, I asked God to please take my life. He could accomplish this through an automobile accident, so no one would know. I just wanted to stop hurting. Then He spoke this question into my heart: "Who will raise your children?"

Good grief, it would be the "other woman"!

Then I heard a little chuckle, as He said, "I'm not finished with you yet." That settled the issue. I was in this for the long haul.

At that time I was employed by the Sparrow law firm, which was composed of outstanding men of integrity. I had previously worked for Don for several years before he joined this particular firm, and he was especially helpful in giving me insight regarding my personal negotiations with Bob. Attorney George formally represented me, and his patience went beyond all limits. He and Bob's attorney at last reached a settlement, but when the agreement was presented to me for signature, I could not sign it. The paper actually felt hot to the touch, and I could not bear to hold it in my hands.

I discussed the matter with my son Steve, and his advice was that I not help his dad with this divorce; that I was not to sign. Bless Attorney George, because he did not choke me for rejecting his hard work but told Bob's attorney I could not sign as a matter of principle. And then George told me he didn't know anything else to do, as he had done all he could for me. Indeed he had, and I was grateful. I really needed a miracle here!

A few months earlier I had been at a point of deep despair. I felt that my faith was weak, and I was going to fail my God. I had also been praying the words from the hymn, "I Am Thine, O Lord " (Fanny J. Crosby, 1875):

> I am thine, O Lord, I have heard thy voice,
> and it told thy love to me;
> but I long to rise in the arms of faith,
> and be closer drawn to thee.
> Consecrate me now to thy service, Lord,
> by the power of grace divine;
> let my soul look up with a steadfast hope,
> and my will be lost in thine.

Another attorney friend of mine, Fred, called me the evening after my meltdown, saying he had a word for me from the Lord, but he did not know how to do it. I asked if he had written it down, but he replied, "No, I have it memorized."

I exclaimed, "Then just tell me!"

And he repeated the words of the Lord to me: "You are my faithful servant in whom I am well pleased. I will not fail you, nor you Me. Let your soul look up with a steadfast hope, and your will be lost in Mine."

This addressed my concern that I would fail Him, and repeated the same words I had been praying. Only God knew, and He used Fred to encourage me.

And He again used Fred to rescue me. He called to say that the Lord wanted him to represent me in my case, without charge, but he knew this would not be ethical since George was my attorney. I explained the settlement situation, and that George would be relieved inasmuch as he had done all he could to no avail. Fred entered into new negotiations with Bob's attorney, and I was surprised that his attorney wanted to take my deposition. It seemed unwise to me on Bob's part to have my incriminating testimony in the record, but God had something to show me. He would not waste anything!

Bob's twin sister Barbara and I had talked and prayed together almost daily since Bob's departure. She and I had sat on the grassy bank beside our pond and prayed the prayer of agreement set forth in Matthew 18:19: "If two of you shall agree on earth as touching anything that they shall ask, it shall be done for them of my Father which is in heaven." The fly in the ointment was Bob's free will.

Barbara was especially praying for me because I was nervous about the deposition. She called me with a message from God. She said the Lord told her that I was "as delicate as a rose, but strong as iron." Meanwhile, my prayer warriors at St. Andrew were interceding, and as I approached Fred's office, I could feel myself being lifted up, undergirded with strength, and it was not my own.

Fred had a short conference with Bob's attorney before the deposition began, at which time his attorney expressed his wonder that Bob would choose this "other woman," who seemed so intent on keeping her hand on every dime he had. God's Word says that He will even make our enemies be at peace with us (Prov. 16:7), so it was not surprising that the attorney was very gracious in his questioning and tried to put me at ease.

At a later date, the court reporter at the deposition came on another matter to the law office where I was employed. She warmly greeted me and expressed her sympathy. Through this particular experience, I learned the power of prayer and the faithfulness of God's Word. Jesus is an outstanding Advocate!

Fred later counseled me to sign the revised agreement because under the laws of our state, the divorce would be granted. If I were to go to trial, certain benefits for the children, including college educations, would not be guaranteed. He refused to ask for attorney fees, thereby resulting in more child support and alimony for me. Barring a miracle, it was just a matter of time before the ax fell.

Meanwhile, life marched on, and daily chores had to be done, including taking out the trash. We had a dumpster at Estex, where Bob would take our household garbage. I continued this practice in order to save money, but I went after office hours. One particular evening, Bob and Maxine were still at Estex; I could see them through the big windows. I hastily threw in the trash and headed for home. When I arrived, my mother-in-law was there for a visit, so I had to remain calm and collected. After she left, I told the kids I was going to shower and they needed to get ready for bed. I took one of my "hour showers" so I could cry and not be heard. It seemed my hopes of reconciliation were "trashed." When at last I retired for the night, I was still weeping. And then I felt my tender Father God take me in His arms, cradling me against His chest. I was wrapped in His blanket of love and peace and slept like a baby.

Chapter 9

The Dreaded Divorce

On February 5, 1980, the divorce was granted. The judge ordered that "the marriage contract heretofore entered into between the parties to this case, from and after this date be and is set aside and dissolved as fully and effectually as if no such contract had ever been made or entered into, and the Plaintiff and Defendant, formerly husband and wife, in the future shall be held and considered as separate and distinct persons altogether unconnected by any nuptial union or civil contract whatsoever."

How can a judge by the stroke of a pen dissolve a marriage? It is not like pouring salt on a slug or throwing water on the wicked witch in Oz. How can you separate when you have been one flesh for twenty-eight years and have produced offspring together? Where is the spout that turns off the love in your heart? It's absurd!

In my prayer time, again came Psalm 91:10, saying that the evil would not befall me. I cried out, "Lord, I am divorced! The evil did befall me, and the plague came nigh my dwelling."

He replied, "The evil did not befall you. You're still standing, aren't you? The plague has been removed from your dwelling."

It was so clear from God's viewpoint, but so contrary to my thinking. To me, divorce was the plague, but to God, an unbelieving, adulterous husband was the plague. On the day Bob left, the Lord had promised me a good marriage; and I had my rainbow, my ring, and a love in my heart that would not die. This could not be the end of the matter.

There is the story of a man who was to meet some friends at a play. He had never been to a live performance and arrived late, slipping into his seat and nodding to his friends. At the end of the second act, everyone stood up, so he apologized for his tardiness and began telling them good-bye. They told him he could not leave then because it was only the intermission. The best part, the finale, was yet to come. Was I mistaking the intermission for a finale?

Actually, I confess here that I never got the hang of divorce. My former sister-in-law tried to explain it to me: when you get divorced, you leave. But how do you leave when the children you both love graduate, get married, have babies, and go through their crises? There was also the belief that he was coming back buried deep inside the core of me. Divorce is complicated.

Bob married Maxine on Valentine's Day 1980. Funny, but no one had to tell me. Friends had sent flowers to my office, and my friend Don, our firm's real estate attorney, asked me to assist him in a loan closing at a downtown Atlanta bank. This was exciting, as it involved a car dealership and a lot of money. We ran into a hitch, and the dealer had to run down the street to another bank to obtain additional funds, which required the preparation of more loan documents on site.

As I was driving home from my exhilarating day, the thought came, "Bob got married today." My mother-in-law, who lived next door, brought us a lemon pie for supper, but said not a word about Bob's marriage. The next day, Barbara called to tell me the news, but it was not news to me. For many years afterwards, Valentine's Day was a special event, as the Lord would give me little surprises to show His love.

It was painful to tell my kids that their dad had remarried. Stacey dissolved into tears and fell into my arms. She cried, "I thought he was coming home."

I sadly replied, "So did I."

One wound she carried for years was a distrust of men. She had many boyfriends, and there were several marriage proposals. The one she chose as her husband learned through experience that she requires reinforcement, and it pleases me when I hear his compliments and praise of her, his assurance that he is in their marriage for life, no turning back. She is loved and treasured.

My sons did not say anything; they just stuffed their emotions. Steve had Brenda for comfort, and I was so glad. He also had been in the trial for two years before us, and he was older now. That did not make the pain any less, but I believe it gave him a determination to have a good marriage for himself. At a later date he told me that in addition to loving Brenda, she was also his best friend and he could never hurt her.

However, Scott seemed to have no one. He had two separate outbursts, and we had long talks, sitting on the floor, face-to-face, weeping. He thought no one cared, no one loved his dad but him, because we were not sharing our feelings. Scott felt he had been robbed of his father. Steve, because of his age, had his dad longer, and when Steve tried to help Scott, he was met with resentment and anger. When I explained to Scott that we were all hurting but handling the pain in our own distinct ways, it made him feel better. He was not alone; we were all shipwrecked! The fact that I continued to love Bob gave them the freedom to never stop loving either, because they did not have to choose sides.

The divorce was perplexing, since I had all these words and confirmations from God that it just was not supposed to end this way. Well, I wondered, maybe I had been talking to myself, missed the Lord somehow. Bob did have a free will. Was there someone else for me? And in my confused state of mind, Satan tried to pull a little trick on me.

I was at the mall one evening and ran into an old friend from school. He looked very dashing in his state patrol uniform and invited me to have coffee. As we talked, he recalled how we would dance together in high school and how I fit right under his arm. He shared that he was married, but he and his wife had "an arrangement." She did her thing, and he did his. I had to stifle my laughter. "Old devil, you'll have to do better than this to lead me into temptation!" I said under my breath.

He said he would call me later for lunch, but when he did, I made an excuse, and he could see I was not interested. My boss, Bill, told me I could go out with this guy one time, but I protested. One time was one time too many. I knew the pain of an unfaithful husband, and I would never be a party to inflicting that agony on his wife.

One day I received a call from a friend of mine, inviting me for lunch. I knew her situation—she was having an affair with a married man. While I loved her, I hated what she was doing, but I agreed we would meet at a local cafeteria. We were there from lunch to supper as she shared how miserable she was in this relationship. All the while, I was questioning God. I was the last person on Earth who should be talking with her. I had absolutely no sympathy for her being this "other woman," even though she was my friend. But as she talked, I could see the love in her heart, wrong as it was, for this married man. Still, as a Christian she had no choice but to be obedient to God's Word. I told my friend that she was robbing this man's wife and his son, and that is what Satan does. He "steals, kills, robs and destroys" (John 10:10). I knew the pain of an unfaithful husband, and so did my children. Finally, I told my friend that I had no more to say. She was headed for hell because the Bible says that adulterers will not inherit the kingdom (1 Cor. 6:9–10). I was emotionally spent; why did she call me? But God does not waste anything! She repented, broke off the relationship, and within the year she met a fine Christian man. They married and are living happily forever after!

I wondered if I would ever be truly happy again. Others seemed to be doing well, but for me life was so daily and so hard. I continued to take hour showers so the kids would not see me cry. This was that yucky part called "walking through the valley" (Ps. 23:4), but it does "come to pass" (Luke 2:1), and "yucky" does not last forever. It just seems that way.

Chapter 10

Blessings from Sweden

My daughter Stacey has "travel-itis," which is an urge to go to new places, meet new people, and do new things. (I think she inherited it from me.) During her junior year of high school, she elected to be a summer exchange student in Sweden. Bob gave her the choice of this trip or a car; she chose the trip. Her reasoning was that since she was a girl, the guys she dated would have cars, so a car was not really a necessity. Sweden was! She came home grownup, not my little girl who left. New cultures and new countries do expand a person.

But that led to another eventful decision—to have an exchange student live with us, not just for the summer but for the entire school year. I admit that I caved in on this one, because I knew it would tear my heart out to say good-bye. (And that proved to be the case). Anna, from Goteborg, Sweden, came to share our lives for the school year of 1981–1982.

Stacey was still in another part of Sweden finishing her tour when Anna arrived at the Atlanta airport. If she had not been the exceptional person she was, I am sure she would have gotten right back on that plane and gone home, because she was met by Steve and Scott, my teenage boys, and they were a bit rambunctious. We needed Stacey as a stabilizer. She did come home about two weeks later, and surprisingly, Anna, who had seen only pictures of Stacey, spotted her on the concourse train when we went to meet her at the airport. Stacey was not on her scheduled flight because she had given her seat to another student, who needed to make travel connections. She had to take a later flight, so we were frantically searching for her.

Our next-door neighbors had an exchange student from Finland, so Maria and Anna were a comfort to each other. They were the hits of the high school. We are a Christian family, very active in church, so Anna was exposed to a very different belief system. She was agreeable to any plan we proposed, wanting to squeeze everything she could from her experiences. Christmas was amazing, as we combined our traditions with hers. We went to a church in Atlanta for a Swedish celebration of light in the darkness of winter. Anna was in a company of young women who quietly entered the dimly lit sanctuary. She wore a white robe and an evergreen wreath with white lighted candles atop her lovely blonde hair. It was an inspiring scene.

Our American Christmas consisted of stockings by the fireplace, a huge Christmas tree, and presents spilling out into the middle of the living room floor. Santa gave Anna and Stacey matching pajamas. Of course, there were the traditional family parties, with singing and laughter and good Southern cooking.

In March we had an ice storm, and schools were closed for five days. Our home in the woods was like a fairy land, and we were all excited about being housebound, playing in the snow and ice, and making snow ice cream. Anna just shook her head in disbelief. This was the ordinary in her world, not the extraordinary!

We went to the World's Fair in Knoxville, Tennessee, in the spring of 1982, with the Rodriguez family, for an unforgettable trip. We camped in order to save money and arrived at our campsite at night. The following morning we discovered we had pitched our tents in the road. Later there was a hilarious meeting, where Linda and I were to rendezvous with the kids at the "finger sign" on the main street. We were looking for an actual finger pointing into the air, but it was only a sign painted on a wall to go "this way." They finally found us, frustrated and confused, and for some reason, this struck their funny bones, as if they needed a valid reason to have teenage laughing fits.

We took another short trip to Madison, Georgia, to see an Andrew Wyeth exhibit, and on the way home Anna stopped by the road to pick cotton bolls. Anna is an artist. She sculpts and designs jewelry, and at the present time, she teaches art in Goteborg.

She loved to eat little trees (broccoli), and on her

birthday in April she requested her favorite meal of fish, boiled potatoes, and little trees, along with her cake. We blended Sweden and America.

Anna occasionally spent time with Bob, and on Father's Day she was invited for the weekend, but Stacey and the boys were not included. When Bob returned Anna to his parents' home next door, Stacey refused to go see him. Later I called Bob and told him that Stacey would come if invited, and he was surprised, because he thought she did not want to come, yet no invitation came.

About two weeks before Anna's departure, her family, consisting of Dad Tage, Mother Monica, and Brother Martin, came for a visit. We welcomed them with a special supper, and as her family waited in the living room for us to get the food on the table, Monica was squealing as she pointed at our big front windows. She was seeing little lights throughout the woods! They were lightning bugs, so common down South. The boys ran out and caught a few in a glass jar, so she could see this amazing phenomenon.

Our world is such an interesting place! I wonder what our Lord was thinking on the day He created lightening bugs; He must have been in a playful mood.

I wrote a poem along these lines:

> What were You thinking of, Lord, when You made
>   the rose?
> From bud to full bloom in beauty it unfolds.
> What were You thinking of, Lord, when you made
>   the tree?
> From acorn to sapling to spreading canopy.
> I look all around me at Your creation,

the glory of your people in every nation.
I see your blessings of mercy and grace
poured out lavishly on every race.
and I stop and wonder and have to ask,
What were You thinking of, Lord, when You made
me?
Am I delicate as a rose, or mighty, as a tree?
No, Lord, I'm just me.
But I'm an original—one of a kind,
and I love You, Lord, with all my heart, soul, and
mind!

This visit was stressful for me because of finances. It had been a struggle to provide for another teenager, and now I had three more adults to house, feed, and entertain. I had tithed since I was sixteen and did not intend to stop now. It was tempting just to "owe" God and use that money for expenses, but that would have been a huge mistake. I had to keep Him first, and trust He would add (Matt. 6:33). And He did!

I received notice from the mortgage company that my next payment was due two months later, that I did not owe for the coming month! They claimed I had paid a month in advance. I called to argue the point, but they insisted they were correct. I considered it a God-thing. I was able to take the whole "kit and kaboodle" of us to an Atlanta Braves baseball game.

We also went to the fabulous Fox Theater to see *That's Entertainment*, and when we left the theater, it started to rain. Anna, Tage, Martin, and the kids were all dancing and "singing in the rain." We had a delightful time, but then it was suggested we go to the revolving restaurant at the top of the Hyatt for dessert. I was in desperate straits here, as I did not have the money for this splurge; I did have a checkbook, but limited funds. How could I possibly say we could not go? This was a once-in-a-lifetime event.

I remember a story told by Mark Lowry about surviving a hurricane. He was staying in a boat tied up at the dock, and the winds were horrendous. The next morning it was calm, the storm had passed, and all was well. He said that if he had known how it was going to turn out, he would have enjoyed it more. I would have enjoyed the top of the Hyatt more if I had known that Tage would insist on paying the bill!

Tage also told me that he and his family planned to rent a car, drive to Chattanooga, Tennessee, and see the sights there for the next week. They would come back to my house for just the couple of days before returning to Sweden. During that time, I would receive another paycheck, so all was well. All was well, indeed!

Tage and Monica came to church with us and attended my Sunday school class. We also held hands and said grace before each meal. I had an opportunity to spend some time with Monica on a trip to Stone Mountain. She had some issues with her father, so we talked about forgiveness. She wrote me later telling how our blessing before the meals touched her heart. I wanted so much for all of them, especially Anna, to have a personal relationship with Jesus before they left America, but that was not to be. Anna said she was too intellectual, and while it seemed to work for us, it was not for her.

She visited us several times in later years, the first time being when Stacey was in the homecoming court for the Peach Bowl in Atlanta. Anna went to the gala events and the football game. I was able to meet with Anna and her fiancé and later husband, Branko, in Amsterdam during a layover on one of my mission trips. Several years later, she visited us with their daughter, Smilla. I thought being a mother would soften her heart toward God, but not yet. On the way to the airport on one of those visits, I told her about the rapture of the church and asked if during her lifetime we should all suddenly disappear, would she think back on the things she learned with us, realize it was all true, and ask Jesus to come into her heart? She promised she would, and so I continue to pray for my Swedish daughter and her family. After all, the Lamb is for the house (Acts 16:34), and I am her American Mom.

Chapter 11

Literally Going on with Life

I TRIED TO PICK up the pieces of my life, to become the "separate and distinct" person the judge had decreed in his order.

My financial situation at that time forced me to seek full-time employment, and I was blessed to again work for Attorney Bill, an old friend from a previous law firm who was now in private practice. He was very lenient, allowing me to attend special events at Scott and Stacey's high school. Bill said things always were better when I was around, but I believed the opposite was true. He was the greater blessing to me.

Steve was attending Georgia State University, commuting from home and working part-time at United Parcel Service.

Upon graduation he went full-time, and one year later, he married his sweetheart, Brenda. In the fullness of God's time, I was blessed with grandchildren: first Ryan, second Jason, third Matthew, and fourth Kaitlin ("Katie").

We were crushed when Jason lived only fifteen minutes after birth because his little lungs were not fully developed. This was beyond my comprehension. Here was a child already loved, who would be raised "in the nurture and admonition of the Lord" (Eph. 6:4). I personally knew of the abortion of an unwanted child close to our family. Why couldn't God take that one and spare our Jason? I needed an answer, and He reminded me of David and his battle with Goliath in 1 Samuel 17. David recalled his defeat of the lion and the bear (v. 36), and, therefore, took courage that he would defeat Goliath as well. I was to recall my past experiences. God had never failed me; He would not do it now.

And then there was this further word: "You are to stand before Me with your hands wide open, allowing Me to pluck out what I want to pluck out, and to add what I want to add. You are to trust Me in this."

Whether it is minutes or years, He is the God of time. Just as in 1978 I had to release my dad, this time I had to release Jason.

In 2001 on a mission trip to China, I had the honor of meeting a law student named Jasson at a student coffee shop on a campus in Xining. He wanted to practice his English, and when he learned I was a legal secretary, he was especially intrigued because he wanted to become an attorney. It is against the law to evangelize in China; however, if the other person initiates the conversation, you are free to respond.

About a week after our first meeting, Jasson approached me in the park. Through a God-incidence, I had been locked out of my room, so I was in the park reading a book. He point-blank asked if I were a Christian, and so I was free to reply, "Yes, I am. Would you like to be?"

He answered in the affirmative, and I was able to explain the gospel and lead him in a sinner's prayer. He was very excited and told me how others had tried to tell him about Jesus before. I was especially thrilled because I knew his roommate was also a Christian but had been afraid to share with Jasson. This was a gift to me from God. He gave me this Jasson for my grandson Jason, wanting me to know He had not forgotten.

Scott and Stacey graduated from high school in 1983, each receiving scholarships. Scott attended Savannah College of Art and Design for a year, and then transferred to Atlanta College of Art and Design, where he graduated, and in 1995, he married Apryle. Sadly and with much heartache, that marriage ended in divorce after five years. Through a unique set of circumstances, God moved Scott back to Savannah. A family needed a personal assistant who was experienced in art and massage therapy, and that was my Scott. At the time of this writing, Scott is an artist and art dealer in his beloved Savannah, having found his calling. As a mother, I am praying for that helpmeet the Lord has in the wings for my son.

Stacey graduated from North Georgia College, and later acquired her master's from Georgia State University. When she was a music teacher at Powder Springs Elementary School and also choir director of Powder Springs Methodist

Church, she called me one evening to say, "There's this guy in the choir." This tickled me because I was not pleased with the other young man she was dating. She married the "guy in the choir," Russell, in 1989. Russell worked hard and achieved his goal of becoming a fireman, like his dad.

In the fullness of God's time, Stacey and Russell became the proud parents of Abigail ("Abby") and later Madeline ("Maddie"). We almost lost Maddie at birth, so we had a heart-wrenching Christmas Day, but in the early morning hours the Lord put His finger in her cheek, leaving a big dimple, pronouncing that she was healed and very well done (like the Pillsbury Doughboy).

Bob and Maxine divorced in 1992 after twelve years of marriage. There were some fidelity issues on both sides, plus Bob had suffered a stroke, so the marriage required more commitment. He had other relationships, but I was not privy to all the details. He was at one point in a partnership of sorts with a lady named Elaine. They lived in a duplex, but Bob did not want to marry again. The arrangement was that if either should meet someone else, he or she would buy out the other. Elaine went to a square dance, fell in love at first sight, and married her dancer. She purchased Bob's interest, so he moved on to new territory.

Since Bob was now coming to more family events, Stacey asked if we could invite him to our family vacations in Florida. I assented, and he most happily joined us again. On one such trip, he told my son-in-law, Russell, that the biggest mistake he ever made was leaving me. Unfortunately, he did not tell me. We played gin rummy together by the pool, but whenever I tried to engage him in a serious conversation, he would change the subject or find an excuse to leave. It was like herding cats—he scattered.

I had always regretted that while all my children were college graduates, I did not have a degree. I set a goal of acquiring a bachelor's degree and a master's before the age of seventy. At that time, Atlanta City Church, where I was a member, offered courses for credit by Logos Christian College, and upon completing all the courses at my church, I continued at the Logos campus in nearby Marietta.

In 2001, at the age of sixty-seven, I received a bachelor's degree with a double major in biblical studies and Christian counseling. The church held a special cap and gown ceremony for me, attended by my family, including Bob. It was fitting that he be present inasmuch as I had a "P.H.T." (Putting Hubby Through), and it was his turn to support me. My kids presented me with a trophy inscribed with the "World's Best Mom, Grandma, and #1 Graduate." This was the only trophy I had ever received in my life, at least so far, and it is one of my greatest treasures.

As Bob greeted me after the graduation ceremony, I told him I appreciated his support, looked him in the eye, and point-blank said, "I love you." His response was a little smile. Rejection never gets easier.

Two years later, at the age of sixty-nine, I received my master's in Christian counseling, but this was a quiet occasion, and rightly so. The first ceremony could not be topped.

I served on my first lay witness mission back in 1975 through the Methodist Church and continue to respond affirmatively at every opportunity. These are mini-revivals of a sort. Teams chosen by the lay coordinator go to churches upon invitation and stay in host homes for the weekend. The format is a covered-dish supper on Friday evening, followed by a song service and testimonies, and then small group sessions. Saturday morning coffees take place in different homes, followed by luncheons for the men and women, with testimonies, then visitations to the shut-ins in the afternoon, and a repeat of supper, singing, and testimonies, small groups, and gathering at the altar. On Sundays the teams lead the Sunday school classes and take responsibility for the worship service, with the coordinator giving his testimony. It ends with another altar call, followed by a covered dish good-bye luncheon. I have been blessed to be on teams led by my special friends, Walt and David, and serve in many churches throughout the Southeast.

Many times on these missions I would give my Isaiah 54 testimony, sharing about my ring and being Mrs. Jesus. The Lord spoke into my heart following one of these missions, and said, "You say you are Mrs. Jesus, and indeed you are. Is that enough for you? It's enough for Me."

I had to consider this, because we are to seek Him first, and His kingdom. He will add all the other things (Matt. 6:33). Did I want something or someone more than I wanted Him? That was idolatry! I repented, big time, and asked Him to live forever on the throne of my heart. It had not been my intention to casually unseat Him.

Walt and David, the lay witness coordinators, also branched out into foreign missions, with David primarily serving in Mexico. Because of their invitations, my borders were expanded, leading me to the next chapter!

Chapter 12

Around the World in Seventy Years

PART OF MY "going on with life" was compiling my experiences on short-term foreign mission trips into my first book, entitled *Around the World in Seventy Years*, which I have previously mentioned herein. Writing a book is comparable to carrying a baby in your womb. Publishing is like giving birth, while marketing is launching your baby into the world.

I shared my exploits in Peru, Mexico, Brazil, Zimbabwe, Russia, Siberia, Israel, Estonia, China, Uganda, Wales, and New York City. It took years to live these experiences and transfer them into book form. It was surreal to hold the published book in my hand on December 13, 2007. The

Lord certainly "is able to do exceedingly abundantly above all we ask or think, according to the power that works in us" (Eph. 3:20, NKJV).

I had prayed diligently concerning every detail of the book and believed the Lord had led me to the publisher He had chosen. When they requested I purchase some copies up front to augment their costs, I was confused. "This is not how it works," I thought, so I asked the Lord for wisdom (James 1:5), and I needed a "liberal dose." He replied that this was not just about publishing a book. His children were fainting along the way and needed encouragement; He would open for me podiums, places, and people, for He had a plan and a purpose.

In accordance with His instructions, I ordered two thousand copies of the book. I was not required to buy that many, but it would not be difficult for me to distribute any number under one thousand because I had so many contacts. To double that would give God all the glory because it would be Him, not me.

There is much entailed in being an author, and I was such an ignoramus! I did not realize that I had to keep books on my book, get a tax identification number from my state, and file quarterly sales tax forms, not to mention the federal tax return on my "business." I also had to knock on the doors for God to open.

My first copy was given to the deliveryman. As he was bringing the books down the driveway on his "dolly," I told him he was delivering my dream. I autographed a copy, "To the man who delivered my dream," and handed it to him. He told me his thirty-nine-year-old cousin had recently died in a house fire, and he was very despondent. I shared about the faithfulness of our God, and he confirmed that he, too, was a Christian. He was encouraged when he left, so the Lord's plan was being launched with the first copy.

Another special customer was Bob. He bought one for himself and another for his neighbor. I did want so much for him to be proud of me.

A dear friend of mine at Bethel Nursing Home was under hospice care and very depressed. I gave her a copy of my book and asked if she would be a prayer warrior for me. She heartily agreed, so I supplied her with my current calendar of engagements, and she covered me in prayer. Upon completion of my assignments, I would report the events. She said this gave her a purpose for living.

My first speaking engagement was to be at a Wednesday night supper at College Park Methodist Church. As I left my home for the meeting, snow began falling. I was already excited, but snow in Georgia is even more exciting. Not many were at the church when I arrived, and the young lady in charge seemed surprised at my presence. My contact friend had called to say she was not coming, and the few people there seemed very nervous. A man came running in, announcing that the slush was freezing, and we must leave immediately. The lady seated beside me quickly rose, got a take-out box, dumped her food in it, grabbed her coat, and was out the door. I told the leader we would reschedule.

The ride home was magnificent! It was like driving through fireworks. The headlights lit the big snowflakes, causing them to shine against the background of the dark night, and they splashed on my windshield like mini fireballs. It took my breath away. I was not upset at the turn of events, because I would have missed this dazzling display of God's handiwork. He does not waste anything!

Because of this cancellation, my first speaking engagement was at a women's circle meeting the next evening at the home of friends of mine, who were sisters. As I approached, Barbara was standing in the driveway, waving at me. I was almost there, when suddenly a huge tree fell across the road, hitting power lines and sending sparks everywhere. Five seconds earlier and that tree would have been on me!

I could see the enemy's hand here, trying to destroy me physically and emotionally with the snow the night before and the tree that night. The fact he was attacking meant I was on the front lines! I was happy to report my close encounters to my prayer warrior and thank her for calling down divine protection through her intercessory prayer.

On many occasions, people have shared with me their desire to write a book. My ophthalmologist noticed my book, and asked, "What are you reading?" I answered, "My book." He wanted to see the title, and I said, "You don't understand—it is *my* book. I wrote it!" Then he shared his disillusionment with his practice, insurance, and all the hassle, and how he had always wanted to write. I told him to go for it! After all, I was in my seventies, and he was just a kid!

One lady thanked me for taking her to Israel, as she had always wanted to go and reading my book was like being there. Another reader said he did not understand why I treated New York City as a mission until he read that chapter. I had been tempted to delete part of one chapter, which described the architecture of a church in Israel in great detail, but my friend said it ministered to her in a very special way, showing her that divine connection between her as a Christian and her Jewish brethren. I had to thank the Holy Spirit for keeping that in the book. Another lady was touched by the Polaroid pictures in Peru. It is exciting to have people thank me for this or that item because this assures me that God was in control as I wrote and I was yielded to the Holy Spirit's dictation.

Many women have approached me following my presentations, commenting on how they, too, have experienced the pain of divorce. It encourages me to hear how they walked through their valleys and emerged as virtuous, godly women. While I would have chosen to never be divorced, it is an honor to share their badge of suffering. It is like earning a Purple Heart from the Lord.

One lady came in late to a Wednesday night supper meeting at her church. I was already speaking when she slipped in the back. She came to me later, saying she was not going to come since she was so late, but the Lord told her to get there. Upon listening, she knew why. She has purchased numerous copies of the book as gifts of encouragement.

I was seated between Keith and Kevin at a ministry luncheon. I had spoken to the seniors at Keith's church the day before. Kevin was a new friend we were both just meeting. During our conversation, I mentioned my book, and Kevin wanted to purchase one, which was easily arranged. He asked about my speaking, whether I was a motivational speaker and what my subject was in particular. Keith answered that I spoke on how God answers prayer.

The fact was that I had shared on the China mission, and many areas had been touched. For instance, how God provided funds, the miracles of salvations, and protection when we smuggled in the Bibles, just to name a few; but for Keith, it was answered prayer.

I have thus far spoken to Methodists, Baptists, Presbyterians, Pentecostals, Episcopalians, senior citizens, women's groups, mission groups, and even the AARP and Rotary Clubs. One place leads to another. It is exciting to see the doors open, but sometimes it is shocking to hear them slam in your face. Still, our Lord does not waste anything!

Through one slammed door, He showed me that I was being anxious and impatient. I am a task-oriented person and want to see the job done quickly so I can see the results. I was counting on one particular church to place many books, moving on toward my goal, but my appointment was abruptly canceled. I sought the Lord in prayer; what was going on here? The Holy Spirit is so wise. He knows all the translations of the Bible, and He led me to *The Living Bible*, Psalm 37:34, 37:

> Don't be impatient for the Lord to act! Keep traveling steadily along his pathway and in due season he will honor you with every blessing.... But the good man—what a different story! For the good man—the blameless, the upright, the man of peace—he has a wonderful future ahead of him. For him there is a happy ending.

I thanked the Lord for this enlightened word to me, and then He spoke further to me in my spirit:

> This is not about selling a book; it never has been. It is about impacting lives. Book signings are of no consequence. You are to speak, and then they take the book home with them. They are my books and they go to the ones I have designated. I said I would give you podiums, places, and people.

I noted that *podiums* was the first word, being a platform from which I was to speak. The Lord was blessing me, indeed, enlarging my territory, and His hand was upon me, just like Jabez (1 Chron. 4:9).

When I was in high school, I had auditioned for cheerleader. The criteria was to compose a cheer along with motions, perform, and teach it to the entire school assembly. Preceding me was the most popular girl in school, and the crowd went wild for her. I was waiting until they quieted, but the teacher forced me to go on stage. They would not stop cheering, so I told them to shut up! They erupted into more laughter. When I started my cheer, my voice cracked with fear. All I could see were hundreds of postage-stamp faces, the most prominent being my old boyfriend, who had just returned to the school, and seated next to him, his new girlfriend. Their faces appeared larger than the others. Needless to say, I was not chosen as a cheerleader; however, the new cheerleaders used my cheer in assembly the next day. The Lord did a mighty work in making a speaker out of me. I do confess that I still get butterflies in my stomach every time I speak.

All my assignments have resulted in great blessings to

me. Only one, so far, seemed very cold. It was following a Wednesday night supper. Christians do love to eat and then meet, and vice-versa. It was a nice crowd, about twenty or so. I was pouring out my heart, excited about what God had done in these countries, but my words were bouncing off the walls around their hearts, except for three. One elderly woman and two middle-age men were engrossed, and thanked me afterwards for making a difference in their lives. The lady and one of the men bought books, for a total of two, which was a bit disappointing. But, remember, God does not waste anything!

Several months later, I was speaking to an AARP group, and here was my enthusiastic elderly lady from the "cold" group. She said it was her job to remind the members of the meeting by telephone, and she had urged them to come because I was the speaker! This was a precious time, everyone so receptive and supportive. After this meeting, a lady asked me to pray for her son, who did not know Jesus. I shared a similar testimony with her, gave her some scripture to stand on, and we prayed together for these prodigals to come home.

It is amazing to me to stand at a podium looking out at God's children and realize that I am a partner in His plan and purpose. Looking back on my life, I see that I missed the first three verses of Isaiah 54 that day in the kitchen, just one month prior to that dreadful divorce decree, when the Lord promised to be my husband. The Lord was also telling me to sing, enlarge the place of my tent, stretch forth, lengthen my cords, and strengthen my stakes. He was breaking me out! There were cities and nations in my future; my horizons were being broadened. I had a story to tell!

When Jesus fed the five thousand with the five loaves and two fish (Matt. 14:17–21), He instructed His disciples to take up the leftovers. He could have simply rained down more bread, like He did with the Hebrew children in the Exodus (Exod. 16:15), but He uses us as His instruments. The little boy with the loaves and fish surely had a mother who packed his lunch (packed any lunches for Jesus lately?), and the disciples were used to feed the crowd. The leftovers show us the value of even the little things. Our God is very economical!

Our God is also very clever. He uses brokenness to attract brokenness. According to 2 Corinthians 1:3–4, He is "the God of all comfort, Who comforts us in all our tribulation, that we may be able to comfort them which are in any trouble, by the comfort wherewith we ourselves are comforted of God." A secular way to say the same thing is, "I know where you are coming from;" "Been there, done that, and have the T-shirt to prove it;" or, "I've walked a mile in your shoes." We take solace in knowing that others have gone through similar situations and have emerged victorious.

People have asked how I got started in foreign missions, and it goes back to the Lord using my brokenness to connect with Linda, who had joined our church. Her husband had been killed while changing a lady's tire on a bridge in New York City. She and her two sons moved to the Atlanta area to be near family and start a new life. She lost her husband through death, and I lost mine through divorce. We were both hurting, as were our children, and our pain caused an unbreakable bond. Linda is fluent in Spanish and was to be a translator on a mission to Peru in 1985. She could not drive at night, so I took her to the first meeting. Another member of the team canceled, so Walt, my coordinator friend, asked if I wanted to take that place. I replied, "I'd love to, but I have no money and no passport." The team sat me in a chair and prayed that if I were to go, the Lord would provide. In less than one week, I had a passport and people were handing me money.

Linda and I would serve on other missions to Mexico and Brazil, but there was an unforgettable local mission where we served together in a unique way. She called to tell me that a friend (we'll call her "Susie") wanted her to visit a man at Emory Hospital, and she wanted me to drive her there and assist in ministering to this man. I agreed, and as I prayed, I felt we should share Communion with him. I took some crackers and a small bottle of grape juice, and off we went to Emory. It was my understanding the man had a heart condition, and we soberly entered his room to find a lady there. She seemed upset that he had female visitors and abruptly left. We discovered later that he was separated from this lady, his wife. We introduced ourselves as Susie's friends, and after reading some scripture, we had Communion, prayed for his healing, and then said good-bye. The next day he called Linda, whereupon it was revealed that he did not have a serious heart condition, but hemorrhoids! At any rate, he recovered and was well enough to invite Linda to go on a trip with him; she declined. I was his second choice; I also declined.

Bertha, my dear friend, served on both the Peru and Monterrey, Mexico, missions with her husband, Haygood. I had included in the Peru chapter the miracle of God multiplying oranges but did not relate her "angel" story that occurred in Monterrey simply because I was unaware of her experience. She told me in detail, and then in writing. Here is Bertha's account, which I have condensed.

On Sunday afternoon our team went to the city park in Monterrey. Other team members and interpreters were already sharing with people in the park while three of us, including Bertha, stood in the background. A young man with blonde hair walked up to Bertha and said, "Would you like to share with someone?"

Bertha was pleasantly surprised and said yes.

He said he would interpret for her. They stopped a young couple with two small children, a pre-school girl and a boy between six and eight years old. Bertha was sharing the gospel with the couple but was interrupted by Haygood, who said they were due at the church in five minutes, and he departed. Bertha explained to the couple that she was to work with the children and must leave immediately. She invited them to attend the service and they agreed. The young man escorted Bertha to the children's building, then he went to the right, toward the main sanctuary. When the service ended, Haygood came to Bertha and reported that the couple had accepted Christ at the altar call. Their children were in a younger children's group; however, the young man was not in the service.

Bertha took the team interpreter outside and asked a small group of teenagers, who had been gathered in front of the church when she and the young man first approached, if they had seen him.

They replied, "There was no man with this lady coming down the street; she was walking alone and went to the children's building. We were surprised she was alone in this section of town because it isn't safe here."

We learned later that this young couple remained active in that little church.

As I reflected on Bertha's angel account, I questioned why this angel did not simply present the gospel directly to the young couple. It is evident he spoke Spanish because he interpreted for Bertha. The answer is found in Acts 10. Cornelius, a Roman centurion, was praying, when an angel appeared. The angel told Cornelius to send for Peter. In response to the call, Peter came and shared the good news of salvation through Christ Jesus, whereupon the Holy Spirit fell on Cornelius and those gathered with him, and they were all converted. Angels cannot evangelize; that is our job as followers of Christ.

In response to the Great Commission, we are honored to go and tell around the world. Angels assist us, and aren't we glad they do!

Chapter 13

Second Wild West Trip

In the summer of 2003, our families decided to make a second trek to the wild west. The participants varied this time. My son Scott was working in Savannah and unable to go with us. Steve and his wife, Brenda, had their three, Ryan, Matt, and Katie (the "Smiths"); while my daughter, Stacey, and Russell had Abby and Maddie (the "Woods"); and there was me, of course. Since physical stamina would be required, Bob was not included. I regretted this, because he had missed the first trip as well.

Stacey and Brenda had everything planned, as it was not to be just a fun trip but an educational experience as well. I could just enjoy the ride! I would not have missed this adventure for all the tea in China.

The Wood family departed first, with the Smith clan to join us a week later in the Grand Tetons. Russell was our only guy, surrounded by his wife, his girls and a mother-in-law; however, he said he liked having me in the van because I would converse with him as he drove, while the other females either slept, read, or did their own thing. We did camp during the entire trip, but it was different this time. We had better gear and a big man (Russell is six feet, four inches tall) to do the work, but we girls did learn our parts of the routine. We helped unload, stretch out the tent, gather the pegs, and generally do as Russell ordered, all with a good attitude—at least most of the time!

Our first stop at a K.O.A. campground was a bit uncomfortable, to say the least. There was a swimming pool, but you needed a wetsuit in order to survive the freezing water. Our campsite backed up to a main road, where traffic never stopped, even in the wee hours of the morning. But these little hardships are a part of the camping life, so we had to grin and bear it.

In south central Kentucky, we stopped at Mammoth Cave National Park, containing the world's longest known cave system. More than 365 miles had been explored, and we took a ranger-guided tour through just a small part. We heard the wind whistling through Wind Cave and gasped at the underground beauty in Jewel Cave. What wonders our Lord has buried in the earth beneath our feet! We are blessed that courageous explorers dared to brave the unknown and share their secrets with us. This caused me to think about certain people who are a bit crusty on the outside, but when you spend time with them and dig a little deeper, you discover hidden treasure.

We continued to Onawa, Iowa, where we drove on "The Widest Main Street in the U.S.A." and saw the birthplace of the Eskimo Pie, and from there went to Mitchell, South Dakota, the home of "The World's Only Corn Palace." I never saw so many things constructed of or covered in corn. We had our pictures made in cutouts of corn stalks, our smiling faces being that "full kernel."

We dipped our fingers into the mighty Mississippi River and rode to the tip-top of the Gateway Arch in St. Louis, Missouri. My Maddie refused to stay behind, even though she was terrified of heights! There was a fascinating exhibit there of the Lewis and Clark expedition. We could have spent hours, but time was flying.

The Big Badlands National Park in South Dakota covers an expanse of approximately 244,000 acres. I could hardly imagine this stark beauty covering such a distance, but it is a fact. Talk about Kodak moments! For miles and miles we saw only the prairies and range land, with signs posted along the interstate inviting us to the famous Wall Drug Store, in Wall, South Dakota, population eight hundred, for buffalo burgers and free ice water. The store covered almost an entire city block. Abby loved their cowboy hats, and we all loved the break from driving, especially Russell.

As we drove on, we saw the granite faces of Presidents George Washington, Thomas Jefferson, Teddy Roosevelt, and Abraham Lincoln staring down on us. There should have been some sort of announcement, like trumpeters playing some patriotic song while drummers kept beat. I had seen pictures of Mount Rushmore all my life, but this was reality—and it was spectacular. We made the hike to get closer views, and we toured the museum. It made me feel so proud to be an American!

We had a neat campsite in an area nearby with a store and all the amenities. Russell had planned to cook hamburgers, a perfect ending to a perfect day. But as we drove in, so did a sudden storm, and tents were either flying in the air or collapsing onto the ground. And then it turned very cold. We had to rebuild our temporary tent home, and Russell grilled on the porch of an unoccupied cabin behind us.

Our spirits were undaunted, and the next day we went to Custer State Park, where we saw bison and the clear blue Sylvan Lake, circled by glorious rock formations. We had supper at the Firehouse in Rapid City, since Russell is a fireman.

Cathedral Spires was a challenge, as was the Rankin Ridge Nature Trail, but so worth the effort. There were mountains, lakes, flora, deer, bison, and even donkeys. You would think, "Well, that's enough of that," but it never was. Each scene seemed to be more breathtaking. As we were driving, a herd of bison came meandering up the road, like they owned it. They did! Everyone stopped, and Stacey rolled down her window, to Russell's dismay.

The Crazy Horse Memorial is also located in this area of the Black Hills. A statue of the Oglala Lakota Indian warrior Crazy Horse, mounted on a horse with his long hair streaming behind him, carrying a spear in one hand and pointing into the distance with the other, is carved out of Thunderhead Mountain on land considered sacred by many North American Indians. The contrast between the presidents at Mount Rushmore and Crazy Horse is that the presidents stoically stare into space, while Crazy Horse seems to be galloping forward into the future. When completed, it will be the world's largest sculpture.

We toured the Mammoth Site at Hot Springs, South Dakota, including a museum built around an active archaeological dig, which was uncovering mammoth fossils. There were skeletons of over fifty Columbian woolly mammoths recovered from the Black Hills. We were glimpsing life as it was on the Great Plains over twenty-six thousand years ago. It was incredible!

We proceeded to Devils Tower National Monument, located in the Black Hills of northeast Wyoming. The Lakota Indians call it Bear Tower, because the deep crevices covering the sides look like scratch marks caused by gigantic bear claws. The tower sticks up like a sore thumb in the midst of low, rolling hills. There were some climbers near the top, but we were content to stay around the base.

The cell phone rang as we neared the Grand Tetons in western Wyoming, where we were to connect with the other half of our family. It was Brenda telling us that the weather had turned very cold and, if we were not prepared, to make a Wal-Mart stop. I had brought lightweight clothes since it was June and to me that was summer, so this call saved me from certain pneumonia. I purchased some fleece pants, a shirt, and jacket, which I wore on top of my regular clothes almost every day for the remainder of the mountainous part of the trip.

My sleeping bag was a real joke. Steve said it was

appropriate for 72 degrees and above. We were happy to see the rest of our gang, and share our thus-far adventures with them. Our Wood girls were ecstatic to see their cousin Katie. She is our little peacemaker; the world is better when Katie is on the scene!

The mountains in the Grand Teton National Park were shrouded in clouds. We hiked there and rode a boat across the crystal clear Jackson Lake to do some hiking in the forest. It seemed each day we asked, "Can You top this?" And God did!

In Jackson Hole there was horseback riding and a wild ride on a slide running down the side of a mountain, and then we all went on a white-water rafting trip down the Snake River, stopping for supper along the riverbank. Maddie was a bit fearful here, so I yelled and hollered as we went over the rough places and were sprayed with water. Then at a calm stopping point, she jumped into the river to swim, which a lot of the grownups, including me, refused to do. She was conquering her fear, and I was so proud. Go, girl!

Our convoy left the Grand Tetons, setting our faces toward Yellowstone. That first evening at our campsite, a ranger came by to warn us that the bears posed a real danger. He cautioned us to lock away our food and not leave items in our vans; we would be able to scare them away if we banged together pots and pans. That night I awoke to hear Russell yelling at a bear while he beat on a pan, and there was quite a commotion. I fell back to sleep because I knew I was safe. The next morning I commended Russell on his bravery, but he was puzzled. I said I was thanking him for chasing away the bear. He started laughing; it had all been a dream!

Yet, Yellowstone was like a dream. The lofty snowcapped mountains, waterfalls, streams, wildlife, and mysterious geysers combined to make a stupendous show of God's handiwork. And, of course, Old Faithful erupted right on time! We were also beginning to thaw out, and life was good until Ryan said that it would be great to have snow. This was a case of "from Ryan's mouth to God's ear," and He obliged. It was like putting frosting on a cake. Our Lord outdid Himself!

Our next stop was City of Rocks National Reserve in south central Idaho, with a pit stop at an old filling station that had donkeys and llamas, of all things, in pens for children to pet. This was a sweet surprise. Thank You, Jesus! The llamas loved our Matt, and gave him many kisses.

The City of Rocks was aptly named, just rocks of all sizes and shapes, and so my Steve, an avid rock climber, was in hog heaven. On our way out of the City of Rocks, Steve thought it would be shorter to take a left turn rather than right, and we got lost. On top of that, Steve had a blow out, which threw gravel up hard enough to shatter his back windshield. Our guys formed a new one out of cardboard and duct tape, and it served its purpose for the rest of the trip. There is no limit to what can be accomplished with duct tape and a little ingenuity!

We managed at last to get on a paved road, and then had another blow out. We thought we could see the Great Salt Lake in the far distance, but it could have been a mirage. It was a relief to finally get back on course and get the spare tires we needed. Fortunately, all our troubles were packed into that one day. God is good, all the time!

At last, my dear friend—Yosemite. Old memories from 1979 flooded my mind, but this was 2003, and it was time to make new memories with more loved ones. It is an odd thing that you can be surrounded with people, those who love you, and yet still be lonely. I wished with all my heart that Bob were with us to share this unforgettable journey with his family, but it was not to be. Take a lesson from Maddie: be courageous, and go, girl!

We saw Bridal Falls, of course, and Glacier Point, which should be one of the Seven Wonders of the World because of its majestic beauty, and Mariposa Grove, with trees that seem to touch the floor of heaven. There was more rock climbing, especially around Half Dome Rock. Half Dome looks just like its name - a mountain dome cut in half with the blow of a gigantic ax wielded by a superman lumberjack.

I was getting a wee bit worn, but Steve insisted I go with them to Vernal Falls. He did not mention that we had to hike over a mile to even get to the starting point. There was a good resting place at the base of the falls, where the water collided with the rocks, forming several rainbows. The rest of the hike was almost vertical, with many uneven rock steps. I told my crew to proceed without me, as I needed to rest. That was the first time I had not kept up, and I felt I was due. They reluctantly went on, and as I looked over this scene, much like that National Geographic from 1979, I saw at my feet three pennies. Some people believe that angels drop pennies to encourage us to trust in God. I had three! That represented to me the Father, the Son, and the Holy

Spirit. I said my thanks to Them and proceeded to take my mountain, just like Caleb took his mountain at the age of eighty-five (Josh. 14:6–14).

As I crested the top, my family was cheering me on, and I waived my hands in victory. The view there was even more spectacular, as you could look even higher and see more falls and more mountains. There was a quiet pool there, so peaceful, and my grandchildren were stretched out on tree limbs hanging over the water, soaking up the sun like lazy kittens.

I was so glad I did not quit. Look what I would have missed! How many times in our lives are we so near victory, yet we lose, simply because we did not persevere, did not go those extra few feet? We are designed by God to be "more than conquerors" (Rom. 8:37), which means we not only win the war but take home the booty. Then we are better equipped for the next battle.

Our next stop was the Grand Canyon, and it was still grand! We established our campsites and proceeded to hike down into the canyon. It was late afternoon, and the sun was beginning its fond farewell, casting its shadows on the rock formations intermittently with rays of gold. You might think you could be bored just looking at rocks, but not so, for the scenes change with each passing moment. I wanted to store the memories in my mind, but we did have to get back to the top before total darkness fell.

The following morning we were awakened very early by huge black crows flying low over our tents, with their irritating "caw-caw-caws." Abby was not only beyond weary but homesick as well and missing her "Kitty-Meow." It was hard to determine whose fussing was more nerve-wracking, the crows' or Abby's. At least the crows eventually flew away; Abby was for keeps! But that was a good thing. I cannot imagine life without Abby. She adds spice.

We left Yosemite on our way to Las Vegas, driving over the "dips" that were so dear to Scott on our first trip in 1979. We stowed our gear and checked into the Excalibur, with its luxurious castle furnishings. I had enjoyed the camping once the temperature rose above seventy degrees, but my body was screaming for a soft mattress, pillow, and hot water. I do love civilization!

We attended an unbelievable magic show, which made me feel really dumb because I knew what I was seeing was trickery, but it was beyond my comprehension. It was all mesmerizing!

We walked down the street to the Bellagio Hotel for a spectacular performance of the dancing waters, combining water, lights, and music. It was like a fireworks display using fountains instead of explosives.

The next day we boarded a pirate's ship anchored right there on the main street, rode water slides at the hotel pool, and experienced some mighty fine dining. Just walking through the opulent hotel lobbies was a wide-eyed experience. Steve did sneak in a little gambling, but very little, because there was too much to see and do, rather than being confined to a slot machine or gambling table.

This was also an educational trip, remember? So it was required that we tour Hoover Dam. It is a striking monument to man's creativity and engineering skill. Security was more stringent this time, being post 9/11, as compared to our first trip in 1979. To see all that water in the midst of the desert is refreshing to the spirit; it speaks of hope. The prophet Isaiah says, "For in the wilderness shall waters break out, and streams in the desert" (Isa. 35:6).

Sometimes it is best not to know the future, and that was true for me concerning Sedona, Arizona, our next site. If I had not totally trusted my family, I would have been tempted to think they were out to get me and claim their inheritance early. I am referring here to the Pink Jeep Tours. Crazy people rent these four-wheeled monsters to drive up and down the red rock mountains, so we qualified. The Smiths were in one Jeep, and the Woods, plus Grandma Betty (that's me), were in the other. My insides, from the top of my head to the bottom of my feet, were jarred, jostled and jiggled all day long. I was bumped, bruised, and battered, but could find no one to commiserate with me. They thought it was funny! Bob would have loved it!

We drove to the top of Chicken Run, where they spun round and round, right to the edge of the tabletop rock ledge. Finally we made it safely to the bottom. I had been yelling all the time, "Have mercy, Lord Jesus," and then I breathed a sigh of relief and said, "Thank You, Lord Jesus," at which time the guys decided we would do it again!

Scripture warns us not to tempt the Lord our God (Luke 4:12), but we did, and thankfully, He was not offended, because we survived. If I were a betting person—which I am not—I would even say He was pleased at our enjoyment of His creation. It was good!

On our last day in Sedona we visited Montezuma Castle and saw the Indian caves where villages were carved into the sides of the hills. We ended our day with shopping in colorful local stores and swimming in the motel pool. The big guys went out for dinner, while the kids and I flaked out, watching movies and eating fast food.

Sadly, the next morning the Smiths peeled off and headed home, while the Woods and I lingered in Sedona for one more day, which happened to be July 4. We attended a free concert and celebration at the Sedona Cultural Park. The Sedona Concert Band and the Flagstaff Symphony Orchestra performed, and, of course, the grand finale was a bang-up fireworks display. It was a glorious happy birthday for our nation. We had witnessed her beauty up close and personal these past few weeks, and my heart was full of love for her and for my family.

The next morning we, the remnant, set out for home, but with more planned "educational" stops along the way, such as Meteor Crater, Wupatki, and Sunset Crater Volcano national monuments, and the Painted Desert. All of these sites are short distances from Flagstaff, in the North Arizona desert, so we were not required to drive long distances off our route.

Meteor Crater is purported to be the best preserved meteor crater on Earth. The tour guide announced that the meteor that crashed there caused a massive explosion 150 times the yield of the atomic bombs the United States dropped on Hiroshima and Nagasaki during World War II. We stood on a platform area looking down into the crater, which is 1200 miles in diameter and 170 miles in depth. There were exhibits of American space capsules, and we were told that on occasion our astronauts train here.

Sunset Crater gets its name from the bright red and orange rocks across the upper portion of the crater. We had to walk on marked trails across the hardened black lava to prevent further damage to the terrain. Forests surround the area, and it is amazing to see Ponderosa pines growing out of the rocks. What persistence!

Nearby was Wupatki, which contains five prehistoric pueblos built by Hopi Indians. Some had three and four levels with up to one hundred rooms. Several blowholes were found, which seem to be connected to a large system of underground fissures. There were exhibits of Indian artifacts, such as their clothing, cooking utensils, bows and arrows, and the like. No one had lived there since 1880.

The Painted Desert was aptly named. It is a vast desert area with rocks of varied hues, much like the Grand Canyon, but flat and spread out as far as your eye can see. It was starkly beautiful—more "eye candy."

We even squeezed in a tour of slave quarters in Albuquerque, New Mexico, which was another one of those surprises. Stacey especially wanted her girls to have this experience, but we were all moved by this vivid portrayal of slavery in our own country. I was brought to tears by the oratory of a young black man as we sat on wooden benches in the slave quarters. He took us back in time, and I was so sorry for the cruelty he and his people had suffered.

My body was moving into sensory overload. What more could there possibly be for these eyes to behold? The answer: Elvis!

The final topping of our trip was Graceland in Memphis, Tennessee, the home of Elvis Pressley. We thought we had missed the last tour group, but Stacey jumped out of the van and ran across the field to the ticket kiosk. Russell was confident. "She'll get us in," he said, and she triumphantly held up tickets as we joined her at the gate.

Elvis was a famous star during my time, but in reality, he is timeless. My granddaughters had a ball touring his home, seeing his costumes and all the memorabilia on display. We had supper that evening at B. B. King's Blues Club—good old soul food, plus music that touched the deep chord in your spirit.

All the camping gear had been put to rest, so we spent our last night in a motel. The ladies were thankful that we did not have to erect the tent and blow up mattresses, and Russell also breathed a sigh of relief.

The next morning we crossed the Georgia state line, and there was the big blue sign with the peach: "Welcome. We're glad Georgia's on your mind." And in our hearts!

Thus ended our second wild west trip. Could there be a third, which would include great-grandchildren? If so, I might consider sitting out Vernal Falls and Chicken Run. But then again, I am a certified member of the C.M.A. (Can't Miss Anything) Club.

Chapter 14

Indian Springs

ANOTHER DEVASTATING SIDE effect of divorce is that you not only lose your mate, but his or her family as well. I had been a Smith for twenty-eight years officially; but Bob and I dated for three years prior to our marriage, so I had invested over thirty years in the Smith family.

Bob's grandmother had been a Jones before she married Daddy Smith, so this was a huge clan. Her father, John Franklin Jones, was a Methodist preacher. The Indian Springs Holiness Camp Meeting began in 1889, and the family has been coming every year for the ten-day encampment meeting in late summer. In 1904, Grandfather Jones built a cottage there for his family. As the older family members died, younger ones took over management of the cottage and organized the annual family reunion on the first Sunday.

I had attended every year since 1950, and because of the divorce that tradition was ending for me. Bob's mother thought she had a good solution to this problem: Bob and I would alternate years. This was agreeable to me, and on the years Bob elected to attend, I would come with the children on the second Sunday, rather than the traditional family reunion on the first Sunday. I confess that I did sneak down some Saturdays during my off years, because I loved the camp meeting so very much, but I would not let anyone in the family see me. I would sit on the other side of the tabernacle, far in the back.

The years rolled on, and eventually Bob more or less ceased attending camp meeting; however, after his divorce from Maxine, he returned to the fold. Bob's father had been in charge of the cottage, but he committed suicide on August 22, 1986, the day before his seventieth birthday. He was suffering from bad health and depression. This delivered a reeling blow to our family, as he was the patriarch. He and Mother Hattie governed, and we all benefited from the fruit of their labor. His brother, our Uncle Maurice, assumed the reigns at Indian Springs and continued until his death.

The family then elected me to be the leaseholder in 1997. I believe the reasoning was that I was neither a Jones nor an official Smith, but just a good neutral who had been grafted in and who loved Indian Springs. At any rate, the Lord answered my prayer because I had volunteered earlier in my heart as I saw the cottage falling into disrepair. We held family workdays on the first Saturday in May for several years, and during that time we did major clean-ups and repairs.

Family members who live too far away to participate in the workdays have supplied resources and assisted in financing other projects, such as remodeling the bathroom (we have a shower!), undergirding the basement, and rewiring. The rewiring was forced on us by a storm but was decades overdue. Our front porch was rotting, so Russell and Steve put in a new one. I am not boasting but merely stating a fact when I say we have the prettiest porch on all the campground. Today, thanks to a family of Joneses and Smiths who love the Lord and are united in one Holy Spirit, we are thriving.

Indian Springs Campground is an official member of the Butts County Historical Society, and our cottage is on their list of homes. The community is invited to tour the campground on the first Saturday of the ten-day encampment, which always begins on a Thursday. In recent years, dates have been advanced to mid-July to accommodate those attending school. In the old days, it was in August to benefit the farmers.

I participated in the first tour of homes because I wanted to hear what the tour guide had to say about our cottage. One thing she mentioned was the sawdust that covered our basement floor, where the children would sleep. I had to correct her, because we had to remove the sawdust, as it was a smorgasbord for termites, and it was replaced with indoor-outdoor carpeting.

When we celebrated our one hundredth year in 2004, relatives from all over the United States came for the glorious occasion. We keep a ledger in the hallway for our guests to sign, and that year we had fifty-nine who signed, some from as far away as California.

Winkie, the caretaker of the camp, called me one spring to inform me that one of the large trees had fallen on the property. When I went to investigate, it was amazing to see this massive tree perfectly placed between our cottage and the kitchen cottage next door, with no damage to either one!

I shall never forget Maddie, my youngest granddaughter, saying it was at Indian Springs that she asked Jesus to be her Lord and Savior, and it was at one Thursday missionary evening service that she answered the call she felt in her heart to be a missionary. My other two granddaughters, Katie and Abby, also have a deep love for Indian Springs. All the girls started coming as babies in the nursery, and as of this writing, they are in the youth group. They have been RADs (Rising Adolescent Disciples), and Katie and Abby served a couple of years as RAD counselors. I have been blessed to pray with them at the altar on several occasions. I am sad that my grandsons have not spent more time at Indian Springs, but we all march to different drummers, which makes for an interesting world.

My daughter, Stacey, and daughter-in-law, Brenda, are deeply entrenched, so we girls have special times of growing in the Lord together as we attend the morning Bible studies and the services of the day. Maddie said once she liked it without any guys cause that way we can walk around in just our towels!

We also have some neat traditions, such as picture jigsaw puzzles. There is no television and no radio, so we sit on the porch and put together our puzzles. When the girls were younger, one puzzle would last their entire visit (approximately eight days). However, as they have grown "in wisdom and knowledge," it takes three puzzles!

We also cook most of our meals, and we must have salmon patties, macaroni and cheese, and baked beans for supper one night. One of the cousins takes one patty home with her! It is also the law that all leftovers from our Sunday reunion dinner remain at the cottage. We would not want to search cars when families depart, but we could!

We do have overnight (or over-day) guests at our cottage, and on more occasions than I can count, I have seen the Lord multiply our "loaves and fish" when we go overboard with dinner invitations. We especially enjoy having the missionaries and their families for lunch so we can hear their exploits firsthand. They kindle fires in us and our children.

I was surprised one year to see Andrew sitting on the second row in the sanctuary with some of our old-timers. He is a retired Methodist preacher, and I met him during a lay witness mission at his church. At that time, he was also suffering the pain of an unwanted divorce. It was good to renew our friendship, and when I saw him pray for a little boy who had fallen and scraped his elbow, I thought to myself how wonderful it would be to be married to such a godly man. We talked a lot that first year. He would sit on our porch, and he ate some meals with us. He said some mutual friends had suggested he contact me. He had been on many missions and was leaving to serve in Brazil with the same leader with whom I had served in 1987. We had much in common.

The next year, he did not come to camp meeting, and then the following year, there he was, coming to visit and rock on the porch. I had built him up in my mind, thinking that with the passage of so much time, I must have missed the Lord concerning Bob. Perhaps Andrew and I could serve as man and wife in the kingdom and truly experience holy matrimony. We had even prayed together on the porch and at the sanctuary altar.

But then a funny thing happened. One evening Andrew came to visit, and Bob was sitting on the porch, enjoying all the good talk, as usual. He had begun coming on the first Saturday evening so he could spend time with his sister Barbara and her husband Wayne, and he would leave after family reunion dinner on Sunday. Andrew could not understand why Bob traveled so much. That was easy—he loved it! I felt uneasy in my spirit, as I did not like his seemingly offhand criticism of Bob. It was not intentional; I was just super-sensitive.

Andrew shared with me later a little about his current life. He had returned from Brazil, feeling his work there had ended, and he told me about his family situation. His wife wanted to restore the marriage, but he believed this would be against Scripture.

There is a special missionary evening service on the second Thursday. My kids love this service, as this is the time support money is raised for the selected missionaries for that year. When the speaker calls for missionaries in the congregation to stand, my kids make sure I get to my feet. Andrew was seated next to me when Abby came and plunked herself between us. He seemed a bit startled but then laughed and said she must love me. I smiled in agreement, but I knew it was because it was missionary night and she wanted to be in the middle of things. Andrew had to leave before the service concluded, so he took my telephone number, which he had lost before. I liked the attention, of course, but asked the Lord to guard my heart. I did not want to even want anything that was contrary to His will, no matter how good it looked on the surface. Andrew had a close walk with the Lord, so I could trust he would be obedient to His leading. Andrew never called.

I take pleasure in observing our family, especially at the first Sunday reunion. We have a short business meeting right after dinner, at which time we discuss any new projects and our finances. They are all supportive, loving, and kind. I sense in my spirit God's approval, and I pray that He lets those family members who are with Him know we are continuing their legacy.

It is sad, however, when loved ones have passed during the current year, and on Sunday afternoon at three o'clock we attend the memorial service in their honor. An especially difficult memorial for me was in 2005, when we honored Wayne, Barbara's husband and my brother-in-law. Wayne was one of my best friends and encouragers; he was my brother-in-love. He would give me good advice when I would call with my questions, and he loved jokes and could tell awesome tales. The family was still grieving, so it fell to my lot, and my high honor, to share with the congregation a few of our Wayne stories. He left such a hole in our hearts!

It is a delight to see the younger ones moving up, knowing that one day they will take their places of leadership, and the Jones/Smith cottage will be open until Jesus comes. I am certain the angels must beg the Lord to assign them to our cottage during camp meeting, because cottage number eighty-three is surely one of the addresses our Lord Jesus gives as one of His homes on Earth!

Chapter 15

Almost, but Not Quite

The Lord had restored Indian Springs to me, and now Bob was living with his mother, next door. Was my miracle close at hand? I thought so, especially when he asked me out to a movie. We dated a bit, but then he invited me on a trip to Acapulco. There was no mention of restoring our marriage, or any talk of forgiveness or commitment. It appeared to be an invitation to shack up, and it was offensive to me. I sadly declined his offer, answering that since he did not have Jesus in his heart, I could not go with him. His view of Jesus Christ at that time was that he was a good man. Period. He had said earlier, when he left in 1978, that he had never believed any of that "stuff," but only went to church to please me. It was evident that he had not changed.

Some of my friends said I should have gone with him, but I insisted they were wrong. I would be separating myself from God through disobedience to His Word, and more than that, I would be setting myself up for more heartache.

I was doing volunteer work with Blood 'n Fire Ministries every Saturday in downtown Atlanta. Teams would take bags of groceries to tenants in the Capitol Homes Housing Project, and we would share our testimonies with them, offer prayer, and invite them to attend meetings that evening and have supper. Our son Scott had a mural in the Fulton County Detention Center a few blocks away, so I asked Bob to go to Blood 'n Fire, and then afterwards, we would view Scott's mural.

My plan was to be low-key at Blood 'n Fire, but my team partner informed me that he did not pray out loud and that would be my job. So much for low-key! That day we had many opportunities to share and pray, and it was not a time to be shy. Bob was cordial with the tenants but very quiet. I thought it was a great day and was especially proud to see our son's work on such prominent display. I asked Bob if he would like to minister with me again the following Saturday, or, I questioned, "Is it not your thing?"

He replied, "It's not my thing, but it is definitely yours!"

Then Satan whispered in my ear, "Well, you certainly have lost him now," and I could hear his sneer.

When we arrived home, Bob returned to his apartment, and I had a little talk with God. I told Him that I would rather serve Him than be married to Bob; I could not imagine living a muzzled life. His Word was in me, and I would explode if I could not be a witness for Jesus.

I had to buy some groceries and treated myself to a yummy yogurt cone. Coming down my driveway, I had to stop before I reached the house because the yogurt was melting and running down my arm. I looked up, and there on the tip-top of my roof was Bob, sweeping off some leaves. I had to laugh. He was not "gone again," and God perched him up high so I could see him. He was keeping His promise—just be patient.

Bob was a member of a senior group and invited me to go with them to Callaway Gardens for a Christmas outing to see the light display. We stopped at one point to visit some shops. It was very dark, and I took his arm to keep from falling. I felt like a schoolgirl in love, and I was glad for the darkness, else he would have seen me blushing. But then we came to the clearing, and I removed my arm from his. I wish I had not done that, or better, I wish he had not let me do that. On the bus ride home, he turned his attention to others, not to me. When he took me to my door, it was just a pleasant, "Good night. Thanks for the good time."

Bob introduced me to a precious couple, Jill and Howard. They were going on a trip to Branson, Missouri, with a tour group, and Bob and I were invited. Howard and Bob would room together, and Jill and I would share a room. Jill mentioned that people in the group were talking about Bob going on a trip with his "ex," and I thought he was bragging about his conquest. I was offended and protested to Bob that I was not an "ex"-anything! I might be a *former.* but I was not an "ex." Underneath the "ex-plosion" was a world of hurt. He just shook his head in amazement, as he had not engaged in any such talk.

We did have a grand time, regardless of the shaky start. Bob and I played cards on the bus, and we enjoyed the scenery and the comraderie. We made a stop on the way to Branson for some dog racing, which brought back memories of our trips to Florida. The shows in Branson were fabulous, family-oriented, and just plain fun. We even went to a lake and rode the "ducks." During a conversation one evening, Howard said he had figured me out. I asked what he meant, but he never answered. Jill became one of my dearest friends. Actually, I think she knows me better than anyone.

Bob lived next door a little while longer, but one day announced he was moving to another apartment. However, I was not surprised. He seemed unable to settle in one spot and made several more moves, not too far away but definitely distancing himself from me. I learned that he had another girlfriend, who enjoyed traveling, and he had been seeing her for over a year. They had made several trips together.

Bob's mother began to decline in health and died on April 1, 1998. I was blessed to be with Bob, Barbara, and Warren (their brother) that day, and as she took her last breath, I called Barbara to come by her side. It was appropriate that her own daughter be in that place, though I loved her as a mother, not an in-law.

Eventually, Bob moved to Mississippi to be closer to the gambling casinos. He was not a gambling addict but enjoyed the thrill of betting, and he also loved being near the water.

I retired in June 1999 from my job with the law firm of Levine & Block, where I had worked for fourteen years. I was sixty-five and ready for a new career. I met Jane, director of Family Life Ministries, back in 1987 on a retreat called Walk to Emmaus. I was so impressed with her ministry that I began making monthly contributions. I had promised Jane I would come in person when I quit work, so two weeks after my retirement, there I was, and my plan is to continue until Jesus comes. Family Life ministers to the homeless, poor, and downtrodden. We are mainly a food pantry but also give out clothes vouchers, household items, and whatever assistance we can, even the jackets off our backs.

Prayer counseling is also offered, and I have been honored to serve in that special way. It is the highest joy to lead a client into a personal relationship with Jesus or to pray with them to receive the fullness of the Holy Spirit, or healing in their bodies. Many times a brother or sister who is a believer is experiencing difficult times and needs encouragement. Of course, the clerical work is important, and sometimes I pray at the desk with clients and put a little red gemstone in their hands to remind them of the blood of Jesus, shed for them because they are loved. Many clients return and show me their gems, which they still carry, and many ask me for one to give to someone they love. But if I had my druthers, it would be to minister in the prayer room.

One day at Family Life, I was approached by another volunteer, a nice-looking man named Roger. Jane had given him permission to ask me for a date. That struck me as being very courtly, so I agreed. We went to a very nice restaurant, and I was fascinated by his life story. He was once a professional baseball player and still enjoyed golf. His wife had died a few years earlier after a prolonged illness, and since he had such a good marriage, he wanted to do it again.

It was a sweet first date, and we went out a second time for dinner and a movie. We returned to my house, and while sitting on the sofa, he took my hand in his, saying what a tiny hand I had. I got very nervous. I did not want him to hold my hand, and I did not know how to get it back! He was much bigger than I, so I looked around to see what I could use to gain my freedom. Of course, all these fears were groundless. He was a true gentleman; I just was not into this dating stuff. I excused myself to get a drink of water, and shortly thereafter, he bid me goodnight. I stood with the door between us, knowing that he sensed my discomfort. We said good-bye, and thus ended my dating relationship with Roger. A few months later he met a lovely lady and they married.

I could count the number of dates I have had since Bob left on the fingers of one hand and not even use all of them. A classmate of mine in our singles Sunday School class invited me to a party. As we backed out of my driveway, he looked at me and said, "I've found the woman I want to marry."

"How exciting," I replied, and then I asked if I knew her.

"I'm looking at her," he responded.

I just quietly smiled at him, but my insides were screaming, "No, no, no!" My son Scott assisted me in avoiding his many telephone calls, and after a while, he turned his attention to another lady in our class.

I asked a male, married friend of mine what was wrong with me; other people remarry and are happy. He replied, "You act married."

And he was correct. When I dated, I felt I was being unfaithful.

Bob still had my heart.

Chapter 16

Presenting My Case

I WAS CONFUSED, AND in the spring of 2000, I took my case to Pastor Rick. I had continued to have heavy intercession for Bob over all these years. He had come back, and now he was gone again. Had I missed God? Help!

I related my history, beginning with Bob's leaving in 1978 and the Lord's assurance that He would be my Son-light, walking with me through this to the other side, promising me a good marriage. I believed this promise, and from time to time the Lord seemed to give me confirmations.

I had a vivid dream one night after praying for God's guidance and wisdom. I was in a village square in a South American town and looked across the plaza to see a cantina with a neon rainbow sign over it. The pulsating colors of red, yellow, and green seemed to be shooting toward me, and I sensed the Lord was in this, giving me His covenant sign of the rainbow. I believed then I had not missed Him; I was in His perfect will.

In September 1999, while serving at Family Life Ministries, a man came in for assistance. He said he had moved to our area from Florida, that he was homeless and had slept in some bushes the previous night. The odd thing was that he was so neat and clean, and he wore an exceedingly white baseball cap. Homeless people are generally unkempt, rather dirty and disheveled. In the prayer room, he shared his story with me, saying he had left Florida to avoid conflict. He was a Spirit-filled man who loved God, but he had not consulted Him regarding his move; he left in haste and anger. His last name was interesting to me because it was Jewish and from the priestly tribe of the Levites. He then looked at me intently, asking if I had a son who had a new truck. I told him, "That was my son-in-law, and he just purchased a new truck; you could use it, but only if he drove." He then said a man was standing behind me, with white hair, and he was retired. That would have been Bob, but I said we were divorced. Then he said that Bob would be coming back.

Shortly after this encounter, I went on a lay witness mission to Union, South Carolina. It was dark when we left the church that Friday evening to go to our host home. I could not see the street signs, but just followed our host. When we ate breakfast the next morning, I was amazed to see that their dishes were my same wedding pattern—an unusual yellow and brown plaid. The husband had us follow him to the church so we would not get lost. The street we were on bore the same name as the client at Family Life who said Bob was coming home. At the ladies luncheon, my friend Margaret was leading, and I thought she was in error, talking to these blue-haired ladies about prophecy. But as she continued to speak, I felt it was all for me, and the Holy Spirit was beating inside my heart. Margaret finished speaking and looked at me, saying, "Betty, do you have anything to add?" The team members started to laugh, because for a few minutes I was speechless. They had never seen me at a loss for words. And then I shared my story about prophecies I had received concerning Bob.

The previous November, I was at an intercessory prayer meeting at Penny's house when a friend of hers, Danita, came to join us. She looked at me and said, "You know that your husband is coming back, don't you?"

I said, "Yes."

She replied, "It will be a short time. Bob will flow with the Holy Spirit. Plan a Holy Ghost wedding." So I planned a Holy Ghost wedding, with everyone dressed in pastel colors. I asked the Lord if it met with His approval. He replied that He liked it the first time. Then I realized our first wedding had the same color theme. I believed that in God's eyes, that first marriage was still valid.

A few weeks later, on a Saturday night, I told the Lord I did not want to go backwards in my walk or lose my intimacy with Him. I would rather not be married than have that happen, that Bob's return would be difficult.

The next day, Sunday, I was assisting in the Communion service at church. My friend Chip was seated behind me, and I felt he had a word for me from the Lord but I did not say anything. As I passed the Communion elements to him, he looked up at me and said, "You have a deep heart issue. The Lord wants you to know this will not be a difficult thing. It will be an easy thing. He does not want you to worry about it."

There had been numerous occasions when friends would give me encouraging words, and I would have those lightbulb moments. At other times, certain lyrics would penetrate my heart, and I briefly shared some of these with Pastor Rick. His advice was that it surely looked like God was in all of this, but it is the Holy Spirit's job to fulfill prophecy. I was to fast, pray, and intercede for Bob but not do anything to make this happen. I agreed.

I shared with my intercessory prayer buddies the certain prophecies and the advice from Pastor Rick. They sat me in a chair, laid hands on me, and prayed. Jennifer said she saw me walking with Jesus and she could see His footprints in the sand. My feet were walking in His footprints, and He was happy and laughing. All along our way were little surprise boxes, which contained things for which I had been praying a long time. This meant a lot to me because I had been very concerned about staying in the center of God's will. Also, in prayer I had sensed the Lord's joy and excitement over what He was doing—like He could not wait, could not keep His mouth shut! Then Jan said the Lord was rejoicing over me with singing (Zeph. 3:17). Penny saw a cross with a red curtain behind it, and on the cross was a golden wedding band with diamonds. She said the Lord wanted me to believe and not doubt, to just accept it and not say anything contrary.

And so my game plan was to keep on keeping on, continue my volunteer work at Family Life Ministries and go on mission trips as God called.

This was hands off, but not prayers off. I would simply go over Bob's head!

Chapter 17

Shouting Time

I DID NOT CEASE fasting, praying, and interceding for Bob during all those years, and in August 2002, I sensed in my spirit that God was moving. I asked Him to have Bob call me if I were correct in this. Bob telephoned from Mississippi on Thursday, September 5, 2002, and before I picked up the phone, I knew it was he. He asked me how to go about getting his membership letter from St. Andrew Methodist Church. I told him that St. Andrew had disbanded but that would not present a problem. He just had to tell his pastor the circumstances. I mentioned that when we had last talked about religion, he said Jesus was just a good man, and I asked what happened to change his mind? He didn't reply. Then I asked him the questions from Romans 10: 9–10:

"Do you believe that Jesus is God?"

"Yes."

"Do you believe that He died on the cross for *your* sins and rose from the dead?"

"Of course!"

"Do you want Him to be *your* Lord and Savior?"

"Yes, I do."

And so, Bob Smith was saved, because "whoever calls on the name of the Lord shall be saved" (Rom. 10:13). Surely there was rejoicing in heaven, and I strained to contain myself. After we hung up, I called everybody, including his sister, Barbara. She called him herself to confirm that he was a believer. In another conversation later, I asked how he came to that point of conversion. He said he was just sitting in his chair thinking about it, and he believed it; and so he did it!

I was expecting Bob to knock on my door any minute, but he didn't. He talked about joining the church, but never got around to it. We are not to judge, but Jesus did say we could be fruit inspectors. There just was not any fruit of Bob's to inspect. Still, this was the Holy Spirit's work. We catch the fish; He cleans.

My son Steve gave me a plaque after Bob left that I have kept in my home all these years. On it is the picture of a little girl with blonde hair, dressed in a pink dress, holding some flowers behind her back. She is standing on the grassy shore, looking out over a lake at a small boat on the horizon. A tiny kitten is sitting beside her, and there is a rainbow and little birds flying in the sky. The message is, "Believe, for your dreams can come true." She was watching, expecting, but the little boat had not yet reached shore. I felt very much like that little girl.

I loved all the trees on our land, but some were posing a serious threat to the house. A delightful husband-and-wife team came to remove approximately twenty-two trees. I had submitted a withdrawal request to pay them from an account, but the money had not come. It was necessary for me to re-fax the request, so I went to my church, New Hope Baptist, to use their machine. While there, I had a chat with a very nice-looking man about my age. Several of my friends were dating, and one was engaged. I was talking to myself under my breath as I left, and jokingly said, "Lord, I think I'll come up here to the north campus (I was attending south), join the singles class, and get myself a husband."

He replied, "Bob Smith is your husband!"

Oops!

Chapter 18

Letting Go and Letting God

On August 31, 2005, a catastrophe struck our nation, causing an upheaval that is still being felt even at the time of this writing, almost three years later. Her name was Hurricane Katrina. The major concern of our family was that it hit shore very near Bob's home in Diamondhead, Mississippi. Fortunately, he was in Australia at the time on one of his many trips, so his safety was not a factor, only his home and possessions, which suffered enough damage to precipitate his return to Georgia. He landed in Griffin, about twenty miles south of my house. He was getting closer to home.

At that time I was still doing volunteer work at Family Life, and our agency was designated as one of the disaster relief centers in our area. We were flooded with Katrina survivors, each one having a miraculous testimony to share. Georgians were pouring out their hearts and pocketbooks, and we assisted over 1,200 families with food, clothes, household items, diapers, gas, money for rent, and whatever else we could find. Everyone needed prayer and counseling. The ministry leases space at the East Point Presbyterian Church, and Pastor Rosie even performed a marriage ceremony, with our volunteers happily throwing the rice.

Our services to the Katrina folks lasted over a year, and during this time my family was applying pressure on me to move to Powder Springs, west of Atlanta. Steve, Brenda, Stacey, and Russell lived within one mile of each other, so I would be surrounded by family. Scott remained in Savannah, so that distance did not enter into the equation.

My neighborhood was being zoned commercial on the highway side, and the area down the road was being inundated with over five hundred new residences. My home was nestled deep in the woods, and my family believed I was in danger. We had some burglaries on our street and even one home invasion, so I was forced to see their side; however, I did not want to surrender my independence, not to mention my dream. Bob was to return home, and that house was home to me. If I were to move, that would mean the death of my dream; I would be giving up—quitting. And you don't lose until you quit.

This was so serious that I *had* to pray seriously! I sought the Lord long and hard, fasting and praying for wisdom. What did God want? I sought wise counsel (Prov. 11:14). Overwhelmingly, I was advised to move to be near my family. Abby called, begging me to come, and one day, Russell called to say that Stacey had been crying because she was so concerned about my welfare. The plan was that he would finish their basement so I would have a terrace apartment with a closed-in garage, screened porch, and garden area. I prayed more fervently and even had a face-to-face, heart-to-heart talk with Russell personally. I did not want to interfere in their lives and be a fussy old mother-in-law, but he said he could only see blessing for everyone. This was so hard!

Finally, I got still enough in my spirit to hear God. His promise was that if I would be obedient to Him in this, I would be exceedingly happy. He was lengthening my cords and stretching out my tent pegs (Isa. 54:2); it was time go (Gen. 12:1).

There were many instances in the Bible where dreams seemingly died, only to be resurrected into something even better. For example, Abraham was told he would be the father of so many descendants that they could not be numbered, comparing them to the sands of the seashore and stars in the sky (Gen. 22:17). When he was so old and Sarah way past childbearing age, it appeared the dream would not come true, but in the fullness of God's time Isaac was born (Gen. 21:5). The rest is history.

Look at Joseph, who dreamed he would be in a position of power with his family bowing down to him (Gen. 37:5–10), but he ended in a pit and was sold into slavery (Gen. 37:28). Subsequently, he was imprisoned on false charges (Gen. 39:20). Famine struck the land, and circumstances were dire, but God used those hard times to groom Joseph for the palace (Gen. 41:41). His dream did come true when his family came to Egypt for food, and they did bow before him (Gen. 42:6). God used Joseph to save not only the nation of Israel but surrounding countries as well. God "is able to do exceeding abundantly above all that we ask or think according to the power that worketh in us" (Eph. 3:20).

The crucifixion of Jesus has to be the ultimate dream-buster. His followers believed He was the Christ, the Messiah, and that He would crush Satan's head in answer to God's promise in Genesis 3:15. The Bible describes Him as being so beaten that he was unrecognizable as a man (Isa. 52:14). He died on a cruel cross between two thieves (Luke 23–33, 46). But, this was just Friday. Sunday came, and the rock was rolled away from the tomb so we could get inside (Luke 24:2). The tomb was empty. Jesus has risen from the dead (Luke 24:6), and He is coming again for His bride (Rev. 22:7, 12, 20)! God's plan had not failed; it worked perfectly.

How many times do we forfeit our victories by not allowing God enough time?

The decision was made. I was selling, and I was moving. A real estate agent who had been recommended to me insisted that I do some repairs before listing. I did as he said, but each time I was ready to list, he added another requirement. Finally, I just put it to the Lord: "You said to sell it; therefore, you have a buyer, so why should I pay a real estate commission? Let's sell as-is." I trusted He would protect me from any major mistakes.

I went to a local home improvement store to purchase a For Sale by Owner sign, along with some pansy plants to put in containers on my porch in order to beautify the place. I had these items in my cart, and as I approached the checkout line, a man stopped me to ask about the sign.

"What are you selling?" he inquired.

"My home," I replied.

He asked me to describe it, and I told him I had approximately three acres in the woods, with a little pond. The house had three bedrooms, and a fireplace divided the living room and dining room, plus there was double carport. He said his brother and sister-in-law had survived Katrina and were looking for a house with land in our neighborhood. We made an appointment for him to inspect my house and then report to his brother.

I proceeded to the cashier but asked her to put back the For Sale sign for me so the man would not see, because I was going to sell my house to his brother. If I were mistaken, I would come back later and purchase the sign. I did buy the pansies.

I had a friend come to be with me for protection, and when the man called for directions, he cautioned me not to be so friendly, saying I was like his mother. I told him I would not be alone. I learned after the fact that my friend, Howard, had a gun in his pocket in case this man tried any "funny stuff."

It was clear from our conversation that the man was a Christian. However, he brought a friend with him who was not sure of his faith, so I was pleased to share with him as we walked the property. I told him how the Lord was instructing me to sell; therefore, I had no worries because He would guide me. We went back inside, and the man called his brother, who was in New Orleans repairing his house. He said if his brother did not want the house, he did. The brother replied that he would be at my home the following Wednesday.

Simultaneously, I was running an advertisement in the local paper and received many calls. I had an offer on Monday from a man who wanted to gut my house, and this turned my stomach. How could he talk that way about this anointed home? I stalled him, waiting for the Katrina couple, Wardell and Marie.

They came as promised, and on that Wednesday after showing the property, we came inside. I suggested they pray about it, and if they were interested, they could call me. Wardell took his wife's hand, saying they had already prayed, and he asked what it would take to get the house. I answered that I did not want any horse-trading, just my asking price. We agreed to split the closing costs.

I had asked God to give my home to the ones He had chosen and confirm it to me. Marie said a family member had a vision that they would buy a home in the Atlanta area, and it would be surrounded by lots of trees. Marie said when they came down the driveway, she was impressed by the woods. When she exited the car and stepped foot on the driveway, the Lord said this would be their new home. What joy! We were all in the center of God's perfect will.

When Wardell and Marie left New Orleans in the midst of the hurricane, they took everything out of their van and put in chairs for their family members. They lost two houses and everything they had, except for the clothes on their backs and those things they were able to pack in their suitcases. Jane had them come to Family Life, and we furnished household and personal items to get them established. I left most of my furniture, and while I was sad when I walked out that door for the last time, I was also glad that they were beginning a new adventure. So was I!

My new home was not finished, so I proceeded to nearby East Point and the home of my dear friend Ruth, whom I had known for many years. We were members of a reunion/accountability group that met weekly. Ruth is a woman of great wisdom, and she taught Sunday School until she was ninety. When her sister died a few years earlier, I made it a point to call her each day. I loved to sit at her feet and pick her brain. Ruth's health began to fail, and during my stay we went to the hospital emergency room many times. Her doctor declared she could no longer live alone, and it was clear that one of the main purposes of my stay was to affirm this fact to her family. Ruth was very independent and would never admit she needed help. She had no children, so her family consisted of nieces and nephews. Her niece Jennifer rallied to the call, and Ruth now lives with that loving family in a beautiful home north of Atlanta.

I wish I could say that I bounced with joy from my old home to Ruth's house, but that would be untrue. The first six weeks were a time of deep depression. I would excuse myself each night at ten o'clock, telling Ruth I was weary and needed to retire. When I climbed into bed, I would bury my head in my pillow and weep. I was homeless, sad, and alone. Then came the second-guessing. Had I made a big mistake in selling my home? What could I do about it? Would my family regret this move? Would my son-in-law come to despise me? Would I be a nuisance to my grandchildren? Would I make any friends? Would I fit in, or just be tolerated? The questions went on and on. I was catching every negative thought the enemy could throw into my mind's mitt.

I shared my battle with only a few select friends, and I know their prayers strengthened me. I also told Barbara, Bob's sister, and she informed Bob. He called me, and I confided my shaky feelings regarding the move. Being his usual optimistic self, he painted me a rosy picture. This was especially painful for me because my dream had died, my home was gone, and it was his fault. His cheerful words, while nice, did not cut it, but at least he cared enough to call. Proverbs 25:20 describes how I felt toward Bob at this time: "Like one who takes away a garment on a cold day, or like vinegar poured on soda, is one who sings songs to a heavy heart" (NIV). Well, you take what you can get!

I attempted to "encourage myself in the Lord" (1 Sam. 30:6) by repeating to myself His promise that I would be exceedingly happy if I were obedient in this move, but more importantly, by reading the Scriptures, which were "an even more sure word" (2 Pet. 1:19). I did not want to just "hang in there," because a friend told me years ago that God's children were not to hang but to stand on God's Word. The one scripture that was foundational to my deliverance from this depression was Romans 8:28: "And we know that all things work together for good to them that love God, to them who are called according to his purpose." So what if I had made a mistake? My God would cover me and turn it all for good. I had to trust, and that was an act of my will, not something

I felt. The decision was made, and I purposed in my heart to praise Him for my new home.

And so the last week with my dear Ruth was a very good week. There was a rising sense of expectancy, excitement, and joy as I prepared to launch into a new frontier. I wanted Ruth to know how much I appreciated her kindness to me, which was above and beyond the call of duty. I knew that she also would shortly make a big move, leaving her home to live with her family, so similar to my circumstances. Our Lord takes special care of His ladies (there's Isaiah 54 again), and we were in His good hands.

With my car jam-packed, leaving only space for me to drive, I departed from Ruth's home on Saturday, April 22, 2006, and arrived at my new home some forty-five minutes later. The whole family descended on the storage facility, where we loaded my household furnishings into our vehicles and brought everything to my beautiful new abode. My granddaughters enjoyed hanging my clothes and displaying my treasures. If I didn't know where to put something, I would direct them to the "technical room," a storage facility housing the hot water heater and furnace. My family made me feel loved and welcomed, and I went to bed that night exhausted but at peace.

I worshiped with my family at Powder Springs First United Methodist Church the next morning, Easter Sunday, and officially joined that day. What better time? I was dressed in my new Easter suit, and this was going to be as good as it would get concerning my appearance. In the following weeks, I visited each adult Sunday school class, waiting for the Holy Spirit to confirm my place, and at last He did. I joined a rather small class, hungry for the Word of God, and eventually I volunteered to be their teacher, with the understanding that I was a missionary at heart and when I answered that call, they would have to find a substitute. They are an extraordinary group, and I am honored to serve with them as we dig through the Bible together on exciting treasure hunts.

I continued to volunteer on Tuesdays and Thursdays at Family Life, but it was important that I minister in my own church, so I joined Maglean's Militia. This is a group of ladies who visit shut-ins and the residents of the local Bethel Nursing Home on Wednesday mornings. I also joined the Prayer Force, lady prayer warriors.

I was snuggling in, doing that "nesting thing" we gals do so well.

Chapter 19

Testing Time Again

My life was slowly conforming to my liking. I believed I was in God's will and had His approval. Actually, I was a bit surprised that everything was running smoothly, like a well-oiled machine. But in short order, that well-oiled machine began to sputter. Our God is not in the business of making us comfortable; He wants us to be comforters. It was testing time, again!

Scott called from Savannah in May 2006 to inform me that he had fallen off a motorcycle and required seventy-five stitches in the back of his head. His friend was driving with Scott behind, and Scott did not have on a helmet. When the friend did a "wheelie," Scott fell off, and his head struck the pavement. He suffered a minor concussion and was badly shaken. Another blow was the shaving of his black, curly hair, but he did look rather striking in the bandanas he had to wear to shade his head from the sun. There were many "headache" days while he recuperated. I was raring to go and nurse him back to health, like any good mother, but he assured me I was not really needed. I didn't like that! He insisted I keep to my scheduled visit in just a couple of weeks. I alerted my family, friends, and the Prayer Force, so Scott was saturated in prayer.

It was hard to wait, but Barbara and I went to spend a few days with Scott, as we had originally planned. He continued to experience headaches but was well on his way to full recovery. He gave us a tour of Savannah, and we went to St. John's Catholic Church. Inside, you feel that you are in Europe in one of the old cathedrals. The stained glass windows, statues, stations of the cross, candles, lustrous wooden railings and pews, and marble floors take you back in time. While not Catholic in our faith, Barbara and I lit candles and knelt to pray at the altar rail. Scott knelt beside me, and I was encouraged, because he had not been active in church for quite some time. When he was in his teens, he had been my prayer buddy, and I missed that!

When we first entered the church, he asked the male attendant if it were acceptable for him to wear his bandana, and the man affirmed that he could, probably assuming that Scott was undergoing chemotherapy for cancer and had lost his hair. As we were leaving, a priest approached Scott, put his hand on Scott's shoulder, and said, "May the peace of the Holy Spirit rest upon you."

Scott was visibly touched, and his eyes filled with tears. So did mine! Here was our Lord again, not wasting anything.

Scott was on the mend, and suddenly it was July and Indian Springs camp meeting time. My girls, which included my daughter, Stacey; daughter-in-law, Brenda; and my three granddaughters, Katie, Abby, and Maddie, were enjoying the second week of the encampment when Steve called Brenda, saying that he had been diagnosed with prostate cancer. This was like a punch in the stomach. She had to leave immediately but insisted that we pray because she knew she would be in a mind battle all the way home. She is a physical therapist, so she had enough medical knowledge to be aware of the consequences of this type cancer. We formed a circle, holding hands (and hearts), and prayed for Steve—son, husband, father, brother, uncle—to be totally and completely healed.

It is so hard to be brave when you just want to cry your eyes out. This was my prayer baby, and the thought of life without him was unbearable. We had been blessed that Scott had been protected from serious injury, and now the enemy was striking at another son.

It was time to put on the whole armor of God. We had linked our shields of faith there on the porch to form a united wall, and now we needed to wield the "sword of the Spirit...the word of God" (Eph. 6:10–18). Our Lord promised to "contend with him that contends with me, and...save my children" (Isa. 49:25). What He had done for Scott, He would do for Steve.

In Isaiah 1:18 the Lord invites us to come to Him and

reason with Him, to present our case. Therefore, I researched His Word and approached Him with three pages of healing scriptures, His promises. To say I "approached" sounds like I just came one time, but in reality I did not just approach—I became a nuisance. Like King David, I prayed morning, night, and noon, and all those times in between when the Holy Spirit would squeeze my heart. Prayer warriors were also standing in the gap for us, and I could imagine the busy scene in heaven as Steve was continually lifted to our heavenly Father's throne of grace.

I had almost a full page dealing specifically with the bones, because many times this type of cancer will spread there. The doctor wanted to do a biopsy on Steve's right femur because it looked suspicious. Steve called me from the doctor's office to tell me I had overprayed, because the bone was so strong the doctor could not penetrate it. This led to a more extensive test, with the good report that there was no cancer in the bone. Apparently excess calcium had formed around this bone due to either a childhood accident or a congenital condition. Another obstacle had been overcome, but we were not home free yet.

On Monday, November 6, 2006, Steve and Brenda stopped by on the way to the hospital for the scheduled robotic surgery. I told my son, "You are going in with it, but you are coming out without it!"

I went later to the hospital, and what a joy and comfort it was to see Bill and his son David. Our family has a unique bond with theirs. David and Steve have been best friends for years. David named one of his sons Steve, and Steve named one of his sons after David. This family was also in the midst of a battle for Katherine, David's daughter, who had been diagnosed with leukemia. We all were wearing our pink bracelets, with the phrase "We're going to win!" showing our support for them. (At the time of this writing, some two years later, Katherine is cancer-free!) It meant so much to me to have them there with us.

Our church youth pastor, Jasmine, also came to sit with us. We met Steve's doctor, and then gathered around Steve's bed, forming a circle of prayer and covering him with our love. We left as he was taken to surgery to remove that stinking cancer!

We were having a sort of pre-celebration there in the waiting room. David and I had each brought a bag of goodies, and Bill had two tootsie pops! There was a McDonald's at the top of the stairs, and David treated us all to lunch. Later in the afternoon, Bill, David, and Jasmine left, leaving Brenda and me waiting for the doctor to come with his good report.

It seemed like an eternity, but the doctor finally came, saying that all went well. He was able to spare the nerves but did shave a little off the bladder, which was a judgment call on his part, requiring two stitches. They would run another count in six weeks, and we needed a *zero*. I just had to give this physician, who had been led by the Great Physician, a big hug! It was wonderful to share our victory with all the prayer warriors, but we still needed that zero count.

I can gratefully say that each report since that time has been zero, all to the glory of God! He truly watches over His Word and hastens to perform it (Jer. 1:12).

The year 1978 had dealt a one-two-three punch, the first being my dad's illness and subsequent death, then Steve's accident, and Bob's departure. There had been mountains and valleys during the years between 1978 to 2006. Loved ones had passed on, including Muther in 1993, which was especially difficult for me, but new loved ones were added, by marriage and/or birth. Such is life.

The year 2006 also delivered a one-two-three punch, the first being the move from my home of thirty-seven years, the second being Scott's accident, and the third being Steve's illness. By the end of that year, I thought, "It surely would be nice just to coast a little bit. Lord, could we have a little breather in 2007?"

I settled into my new surroundings, trying to be a good "tenant" in my daughter's house. I love my home and my landlord/handyman/yard man/whatever-I-need-man and son-in-love, Russell. I have tried to maintain a low profile and not be an irritant, because there is truth to the teaching of Jesus about sitting at the end of the table, and then you can be invited to move up to the front (Luke 14:10).

An added little pleasure is "walking the land" with Russell, as I did with Bob years ago.

Chapter 20

Change Is in the Air

BOB TOOK ALL the fellows in the family on a cruise in January 2008. We had been conversing regularly by phone, and I noticed at Christmas that he was not up to par. He would tell me how difficult it was to get to the mailbox, and he did not have the energy to maintain the house and yard. It was evident on the cruise that these were not empty words. When he returned home, the guys insisted he go to his doctor immediately.

His brother Warren drove him to the Veterans Administration clinic in East Point, where I met them. Warren left, and I accompanied Bob into the doctor's office. After examination, we were instructed to go directly to the hospital. I checked him in at the Veterans Administration hospital in Atlanta, where he stayed that week. Upon discharge, the doctor gave a very discouraging report. The right side of the heart is made to hold blood, but in Bob's case, it was pumping blood, resulting in blockage and hypertension. The blood could not get in with the oxygen he needed. As the heart began to fail, the fluid built up, causing swelling and bloating. He was to use oxygen continuously and continue taking blood thinners. Nurses would be sent to his home; otherwise, he would spend most of his time in the hospital. This was like a bad dream.

Upon release, I took Bob to the home of his sister, Barbara. On our way, he said he wanted to sell his house in Griffin, move close to us, and attend our church. He also asked if I would anoint him with oil and pray for him. Certainly! This was like a good dream, were it not for his physical condition.

I reminded him of Barbara's concern for his salvation, so we went through the questions again (Rom. 10:9–10), and he affirmed his faith in Christ. I said, "Now, when Barbara comes at you, you just say you are saved!"

We put him into bed at Barbara's, as he was very cold, and I reviewed with her all the doctor had said and our plan to get him into a facility close to our family in Powder Springs. When I went into his room to say good-bye, he had the electric blanket as high as it would go and the covers were up to his chin. I approached with anointing oil in my hand, and he was happy that I had not forgotten his request. I anointed his forehead and prayed for his healing. When I finished, he looked at Barbara, and with a huge smile he said, "Barbara, I'm saved!"

The ride home was hard, not because of the heavy rainfall but because of my heavy heart. On the one hand, I was so happy that Bob was at last coming home to his family and that he belonged to Jesus. Our prayers had been answered. But, on the other hand, how long would we have him? I prayed for more time and that it would be quality time. The answer that came into my spirit was that it would be "a while," and I knew he would be gone by camp meeting time in July.

Barbara took good care of her brother during that month of February, but it was up and down. He would have a good day, and we would be encouraged; but a bad day would follow, and we would be discouraged. We were accustomed to a Bob full of life and energy, constantly on the go, but this was a different Bob. All his energy and vitality had been sapped, leaving a body incompatible with his mind. This was especially difficult for Barbara, because her husband, Wayne, had died two years earlier under much the same circumstances, and she was especially close to her twin brother. Barbara and her family took Bob on a trip to Panama City, Florida, but he spent the entire time in the motel room, having no strength to go to the beach or even out to eat.

My dear Brenda, my daughter-in-love (I just don't like that term *in-law*; it's so cold), is a physical therapist, and she had the expertise to know the best facility for Bob. She located Legacy of Dallas, an assisted living complex just eight miles from our homes. Bob said if we liked it, he would like it, and gave us the green light to formalize the arrangements. Brenda and I chose the apartment we thought best and took him for final approval, coordinating his inspection with a doctor's visit and a trip to Griffin to settle affairs there.

The family organized and moved Bob's furniture and furnishings from his house in Griffin on Saturday, March 8, 2008, to his new home at Legacy. While we were moving, Bob's neighbor Tracey came over. She said Bob's "girlfriend" had told her that he was moving. She must have sensed my surprise, because she quickly added that they had broken up but were still friends. This hurt my feelings—not that they had broken up, but that he had a recent girlfriend. My thought was, "What kind of idiot am I?"

As I prayed about this later, the Lord spoke to my heart, "This man will hurt you all his days, but what choice do you have? I am love, and My love is in you."

Then I remembered a time long ago when the Lord promised that each time I prayed, He would fill me with more love, like a car going to a filling station. He continued, "Is it not better to love and risk being hurt than never to love at all?"

On our way to Legacy, we made a short stop at Family Life Ministries in East Point to pick up a power scooter so Bob would be mobile and have access to the dining area and other parts of the complex. Our Lord was providing all our needs (Phil. 4:19), and it was exciting! We were an exhausted crew at the end of the day, but Bob's new home was warm and inviting, awaiting its new tenant.

When I arrived at Barbara's home the following day, Bob already had on his jacket and was raring to go! It took over an hour to get to Legacy, and he chatted all the way. The kids were to meet us there, but we arrived first. I left Bob at the entrance, as I had to get his scooter from the apartment, but my card-key would not open the door.

Meanwhile, Steve and Brenda, and Stacey and Russell arrived; we reprogrammed the key; got the scooter; and the guys went to get Bob. As he drove his scooter to the door of his apartment, I took his picture. He was laughing that great big laugh that seemed to come from his toes. When Bob laughs, you have to laugh, too, because it is so contagious. When he came into the apartment, he stopped and looked around. He exclaimed, "You even got my little brown jug!"

Then he burst into tears, so overwhelmed with gratitude that he could not stop thanking everyone. This was the first time my children had seen their dad cry, and Steve and Stacey were crying and hugging him, with Steve saying, "Oh, Pop!" Bob reached out his arms to hug everybody. There wasn't a dry eye in the place, but they were happy tears.

The hospice nurse came and gave us a rather good report as to Bob's lungs and the swelling. We were introducing ourselves, and it was awkward for me. I always felt married to Bob, and it was hard to say "former wife." She then turned to Bob and asked if he had a good friend. He pointed to me and said, "She's my good friend!"

This team of nurses became a rock we leaned on during the following month. They were tenderhearted and compassionate. To express a need was to have it speedily met. It was so typical of our Lord to give us these comforters.

We stayed with Bob until late evening and worked out a schedule so he would be daily covered during this time of adjustment. Some member of the family would be with him every day, and we would take him to his appointments. It was important that he feel loved, safe, and secure. When I checked on him the following morning, he said he had been unable to sleep because of the excitement. Brenda came by with new bathmats, and Stacey and her daughter Maddie came for supper. Thus, we began our routine.

During the following weeks, we brought in plants and flowers, filled his grocery lists, hung pictures, washed his clothes, took him to the bank and medical appointments, doled out his meds in the correct amounts, and handled his business affairs. He had made a special new friend, Stuart, who was also his next-door neighbor. Bob would read his newspaper and then hang it on Stuart's door. This was another prayer answered—that Bob would have a "buddy."

On one particular day when I came to deliver his "order" from Wal-Mart, he was extremely tired from reorganizing his things. I was trying to help, but he had to rest, as he was short of breath. He kept thanking me, so I kissed him on the cheek and gave him a little hug. Then he teared up and had to struggle to stay in control. This was so hard, seeing him so helpless. He was always so strong, smart and capable. Now he was broken, yet still in good spirits. I, too, struggled to stay in control.

I had prayed that morning, feeling a burden of intercession and asking God who was on His heart. The answer was that it was me, and that He wanted me to "maximize" my day. I had to turn this over in my mind. There is a box on my computer that will maximize what is on the screen. The thing on which you wish to focus appears larger, easier to see. I thought of the scripture, "This is *the* day the Lord has made; let us rejoice and be glad in *it*" (Ps. 118:24, NIV, emphasis added). Just take it a day at a time.

Everything that comes at me is sifted through His hands; therefore, He will ultimately work it for my good (Rom. 8:28). If I would just look, "maximize," I would see His imprint. I had written about this many years ago:

> I see my Jesus everywhere I look,
> I see Him in the flowers beside the brook,
> I see Him in my true love's eyes,
> I see Him in the starry skies.
>
> I hear my Jesus calling after me,
> His voice rings o'er the stormy seas.
> "Come, my child, and follow Me,
> Together we will go through all eternity."
>
> I feel His love coming over me.
> "Lord, make me all I can be.
> Take this nothing and make me something,
> Claim me as a child of the King."

Bob wanted to go to church with us, and on Sunday, March 21, Steve drove his dad to the Easter service. We had dinner at Stacey's home, and our girls looked especially beautiful. There was a lovely picture I captured in my mind: Stacey preparing her dad's plate and cutting up his meat. Bob only brought one oxygen tank, and it was running low, as was his energy, so I drove him home for much-needed rest. It had been a very good day!

A few days later I drove Bob to the hospital for a physical therapy evaluation. The scooter we had from Family Life was getting a bit cantankerous, and he needed a replacement. The nurse wanted him to have a power wheelchair, but he emphatically declined. He insisted on a scooter, as he hated that invalid image, but he did accept a walker. I told him to do as he pleased, because that is what he always did anyway. Plus, I could see his point; a man does have his pride. On the way home, we reminisced about the "Laughing Place," our dry cleaners in Hapeville, where we lost our shirts. We agreed there were no regrets, at least as to the "Laughing Place."

The following day Bob called, apologizing for bothering me since we were just out the day before, but the bank needed him to come in personally. That was no problem, and I told him I could see him getting stronger. One day he would drive there himself, and he agreed. I had felt the Lord's presence strongly on the way to get Bob and sensed His pleasure that I would respond to His interruption of my plans in order to help one of His children. I was to keep my marriage vows, whether Bob did or not.

We were keeping Bob on the move. The next day we took him to the production of *Footloose* at McEachern High School, featuring our two granddaughters, Katie and Abby. We were unable to use the scooter, so he had to walk a short distance, but it was too much. Also, it was very cold in the theater. He was a trooper, though, and was bragging on our "stars." We gave them flowers and took pictures. The girls were so glad he came because it was a great sacrifice—he gave up a Braves baseball game! Our Stacey did some innovative driving, so the way out was much shorter.

The following week Bob twisted his ankle, so the walker came in handy. Here was the Lord again, providing before the need arose (Isa. 65:24). He was making everything as easy as possible, but it took hindsight to see that.

We had a delightful surprise the first part of April. Our dear friend Liz drove over from South Carolina, and we had lunch with Bob. Her husband, Dick, had gone to school with Bob, and had been employed by Bob at Estex for a short while. Their daughter, Debbie, was our goddaughter and lived with us for a short period in 1975. (See Chapter 4.) Liz knew of Bob's affair long before I did and said she told him that when he ended that affair, not to tell me. She knew he loved me and would come home. I asked why she did not inform me at the beginning. She said it would hurt me, and she thought it would soon be over. Bob and I loved that family, and it broke my heart when they divorced. Liz and I stayed in touch over the years. It is one of those relationships that you can pick up midstream at any time and it is as if not one day has passed. We had a great time talking about the good old days, "B.D." (before divorce).

Dick had moved back to Atlanta several years earlier and was living with Debbie. Bob and I visited Dick prior to his last illness, and I had an extraordinary telephone conversation with him shortly before he died in the year 2000. We talked about an hour, as he shared his hurt and anger over his second wife's death. I was pleading with him to accept God's love and comfort by inviting Jesus to come into his heart. Then he said a strange thing, "You almost have me convinced," and said he could not talk anymore.

I recalled Paul's conversation with King Agrippa recorded in Acts 25:13–26:32. Paul had poured out his heart, but when it came time for a decision, King Agrippa said, "You almost persuade me to become a Christian" (Acts 26:28).

Bob and I were to visit Dick on a Sunday afternoon, but Dick canceled, saying he was not well. A few days later he died, so we did not see our friend again. I was grieving his loss and wrote this poem, which I titled, "By Way of the Cross:"

My friend died suddenly today and there is sadness
in my heart.
There was more I had to say to him before we had
to part.
I had more evidence with which to build my case,
But he left me with tears running down my face.

I tried before to tell him, but he just wouldn't listen,
Still, I was sure I had more time to complete my
mission.
He just had to know before he left this earth
That Jesus died for him because he had such worth!

The cross is the bridge reaching from Earth to
heaven.
There is only one Way—not four or five, or six, or
seven.
The cry of our Lord's heart is that none would be
lost;
That all would come home by Way of the Cross.

I pray my friend is with Jesus and the angels in
glory,
Learning with excitement and joy the truth of God's
story.

We are the reason for the crucifixion and
resurrection—
Jesus provided Himself as the Great Connection.

It is so hard, being left with this big question mark.
Did my friend make it to heaven, or did he not?
My soul rests in the unfailing love of my Lord.
Jesus did all He could—how can we ask for more?

I'm trusting in my Lord and in His goodness today,
That somehow He came in time and showed him
the way,
That my friend gladly took the Master by the hand,
And was ushered into heaven's promised land.

A few days after Liz's visit, Bob was having a burst of energy and drove his scooter outside to the parking lot to check on his car. He always had a nice car, no matter our financial circumstances. I teased him about trading one before it got dirty and needed a car wash. I suggested that the next day he go out and crank the engine; however, when the next day came, he had a stomach virus, which kept him under the weather for several days.

And then it was Saturday, April 12, 2008—a day I shall never forget. Bob called just as I was leaving to come to him. He was very swollen and could not get into any of his summer pants. All of his sweatpants and other clothes were dirty. When I arrived, he was eating lunch in the dining room with Stuart, who had spilled tea all over Bob's pants. Then Bob could not find the key to his scooter; it had fallen out of the ignition and was under the scooter. All of this was exhausting, so I got him back to his apartment, put clean sheets on the bed and gathered all his dirty clothes. I found a clean set of sweatpants and a shirt for him to wear, and left him in his chair, watching the Braves baseball game. When I called later, he had slept through supper, so I gathered all the clean clothes, stopped, and picked up burgers and fries. When I got there, I told Bob about his friend Carol's picture, which I found in his sock drawer, and that I had put it on top of the dresser. He said she had called earlier that day to check on him. I asked how she was, as she had lymphoma, and he said she was doing all right.

And then he said, "This is awkward." I agreed. He told me what a fine lady she was, and I again agreed. I had met her before at one of Scott's art exhibits.

Bob took my hand to say grace over our meal. As he prayed, he thanked the Lord for me, saying he could not get along without me. I just squeezed his hand. And then came the words I had longed to hear for thirty years:

"I never stopped loving you."

"Then why did you leave me?"

"Dumbest thing I ever did. Please forgive me for all the hurt and pain I've caused you."

"Oh, Bob. I forgave you a long time ago. I love you, too. I prayed you'd come back, and now you have."

We embraced and kissed, each of us fighting to hold back the tears. How strange that at this climatic moment there were no words, just love, and that was enough. Bob was so emotionally and physically spent that he had to go to bed, and I gently wished him a good night's rest. I, too, was exhausted, and needed some quiet time to process my miracle.

I stayed cool until I reached my car. I had waited thirty years to hear those words, but they came from a broken man, and I never wanted that. I wanted my strong, virile Bob to knock on my door, confess his undying love, sweep me off my feet, and then we would have many more years of wedded bliss. But we were running out of time. I thought, "Yes, he will hurt me all my life, and when he dies, I will still hurt."

I remembered lines from a movie I had seen where the woman is tempted to leave her husband for another man, but she chooses to stay. He said to her, "I would not have stopped you from leaving, but after you left, I would lay down and die." I am so glad I did not lay down and die when Bob left. I felt dead inside, but by God's grace, I kept living, and I have had a wonder-filled life. The Lord entrusted to me three precious jewels, and He has added more jewels along the way. Love is not terminal; it just feels that way.

Bob's condition started to decline even more. Brenda took him to another physical therapy appointment and had difficulty getting him in and out of the car. Russell put a platform on his recliner, as he had trouble with that as well. Brenda advised the family to mentally prepare, and Russell agreed. I told Russell I was trying, but how do you "prepare"? It seems that death is lurking out there, waiting for an opening.

It was Friday, April 18. Bob called around three o'clock in the afternoon. I had been working in the yard and had just come in for a shower. I had talked to him earlier in the day, and he was OK. But now he said he was "not doing too good," and he wanted me to come. I called Brenda and then the nurse. As I drove, I asked the Lord for double grace.

When I arrived, I told Bob that the nurse and Brenda were on their way and asked if he were all right with everyone. "I know we are fine," I said, "but what about the kids? Are you right with them?" He believed he was, and so I asked if he wanted to settle anything else. He made me promise "no hospital," and as to any service, that it be "simple."

Then we finished our conversation of that special Saturday. He told me, "I love you so much."

I replied, "I love you, too," and he held me in his arms and we kissed. I told him I thought when Maxine left, he would come home, but he did not. He just shook his head.

I cried, "Life's not fair! I prayed all these years for you to come back, and now you're leaving me again!"

Then we agreed that we were husband and wife, soulmates forever. I told him that when he got saved, I advised people to fasten their seatbelts because Jesus was coming, and we laughed, but it was so comforting to know his eternity was secure. I had no doubts about that, and neither did he!

When Brenda came, he extracted the same "no hospital" promise from her. The nurse was right behind her and said that his vital signs were good and lungs were clear, but she ordered a nebulizer, morphine, and more medications. Nurses came every day, and a member of the family was by his side until we were no longer needed.

We celebrated our son Steve's birthday that Sunday. Bob only ate a bite of sandwich but all of Brenda's special chocolate desert, and that was fine with us. Our son Scott in Savannah had been bitten by a poisonous spider and was to keep his leg elevated, so he was on standby.

Bob was now stuck with me; I was not leaving! There were tender moments when he would take my hand and tell me that he loved me "very, very much." We had some funny episodes, which Bob described as "hilarium," a take-off on the word *hilarious*.

One time he was sitting on the edge of the bed and suddenly started leaning to one side. I could not hold him and he slid onto the floor; I could not lift him, and threatened, "You better not tell people I pushed you!" But he jokingly did. Another day, he urinated on the floor before I could get the urinal, and I told him that his pride had to go.

On that last day, he wet the bed as I was yelling, "Hold it!" Somehow, I changed those sheets with him in the bed, because I could not bear the thought of him lying there in that condition.

Russell answered our call and was amazed at what we had done. Bob asked me if that day's "hilarium" had surpassed the previous day's. "No," I replied, "nothing could surpass that!" It was our private joke.

Russell bathed him, brushed his teeth, combed his hair, and we dressed him in fresh pajamas, preparing him for company that was coming: his sister Barbara and her daughter, Debbie, and his brother Warren and wife, Sue.

I gave Barbara a tour of Legacy, and she was pleased that her brother was in a beautiful place. She and Debbie left to beat the traffic through Atlanta, but Warren and Sue stayed until the nurse came. She said that Bob was deteriorating rapidly, and she gave him morphine. I had held off because he hated it, as it made him confused, and I wanted him to be alert for Barbara and Warren. He thought his blood pressure signs were great, but they were not, as the numbers were closing in. Then he accused me of giving him morphine, and I could truthfully reply that I did not (the nurse did). Warren and Sue departed, and our son Scott arrived, to my joy. We had called him earlier and told him to come. Bob chatted with Scott. Steve and his son Matt came, then Stacey and Russell.

I had a brief conversation alone with Bob, asking if he had done all he wanted to do. I said, "I'm sorry you didn't get to join the church, but if you want to, we can still do that." He said he would really like that, and Pastor Susan said by phone she would take care of that the following morning at eleven o'clock. So everything was done.

Bob was weary from all his visitors, and wanted to take a nap until the Braves game that evening, when Pitcher Smoltz was going for his three thousanth strikeout. His breathing was regular but heavy. Stacey and Russell left because Stacey had a church meeting. Russell wanted to stay, but he did not want to say he thought the time was near.

The guys were watching the game, and I was seated almost in the doorway so I could check on Bob. I went to his side several times, as I did not want him to miss the game. Suddenly he was quiet, and I could not hear him breathe; I knew he was gone. I gave him a final kiss and hug, told him I loved him, and accused him of sneaking out on me. I looked up and smiled, just in case his spirit was lingering for a moment or two. Then I took a deep breath and called for Steve to come and check his dad. Scott and Matt rushed in as well. Bob left without saying good-bye.

Peggy Lee sings a song called "Is That All There Is?" That was how I felt.

This was a momentous occasion. My husband had graduated to be with his God, and there were no trumpets. At least not any that I could hear. It was so quiet, just a gentle slipping away. But then, our Jesus is a gentle Shepherd.

The silence quickly ended. Family and friends must be notified, officials must be in attendance, plans had to be made, and tears had to be shed.

Life goes on, in spite of our broken hearts.

Chapter 21

Celebration

STACEY ORGANIZED HER dad's home-going celebration, and he would have enjoyed it immensely. I wonder if the Lord lets us attend our own funerals—invisible, of course. Maybe we are too busy greeting our families in heaven, walking streets of gold, checking out our mansions, and not wanting to leave Jesus for a second.

Bob loved to travel, and in the PowerPoint presentation there were photographs of him using every mode of transportation: cars, trains, buses, airplanes, hot air balloons, and even elephants. He was always laughing.

Steve played the guitar and sang "I'll Fly Away," while the Wood family sang "Go Rest High on That Mountain," with lyrics especially tailored for Bob.

Pastor Susan spoke from Psalms 126 and 128, promises God gave me shortly after Bob left that first time.

The family exited to the song "Ain't No Grave Going to Hold This Body Down!" For a long time Satan thought he had Bob, but now Bob and his Jesus were having the last laugh.

There is a family plot in Forest Park where the Smiths and Joneses are buried. Bob had purchased a separate section for his family and had previously offered me a place. I had declined, saying that if he married again, this would be hurtful to his wife. He had emphatically declared he would never marry again, and I had accepted the plot on that condition.

When I came to the gravesite after our celebration service, I was shown my future burial place at Bob's side. He had always been faithful to pay child support and alimony, give me financial gifts for birthdays and Christmases, and pay for my dinners on family vacations. He had wanted to pay for my resting place alongside him, and in the end, he had his way!

I recalled from the Bible poor, rejected Leah, Jacob's first wife. When Jacob gathered his sons to give them instructions about his burial, they were told to take him home to the burial cave of his ancestors, where Abraham was buried with his wife Sarah, and Isaac was buried with his wife Rebekah. He would be buried next to Leah, not the favored Rachel (Gen. 49:31). Faithful Leah persevered and received a place of honor by her husband's side.

A short time after the funeral, I went to the cemetery to take fresh flowers. The old ones had been removed, and the area was cleanly raked. On top of Bob's grave lay a single faded yellow rose. I took it home with me, for I recognized its name: Acceptance with Joy.

My Lord retrieved for me one yellow rose as confirmation that He does not waste anything! He kept every promise and gave me a happy ending!

To Contact the Author

betty@bettyterrysmith.com

Web site: www.bettyterrysmith.com